Methods of Microeconomics:

A Simple Introduction

Also by K.H. Erickson

Simple Introductions

Accounting and Finance Formulas
Choice Theory
Corporate Finance Formulas
eBay
Econometrics
Economics
Financial Economics
Financial Risk Management
Game Theory
Game Theory for Business
Investment Appraisal
Marketing Management Concepts and Tools
Mathematical Formulas for Economics and Business
Methods of Microeconomics
Microeconomics

Methods of Microeconomics:

A Simple Introduction

K.H. Erickson

© 2014 K.H. Erickson

All rights reserved.

No part of this publication may be reproduced, stored in or introduced into a retrieval system, or transmitted in any form or by any means, including electronic, mechanical, photocopying, recording or otherwise, without the prior permission of the author.

Contents

Introduction	6
1 Consumer Preferences and Utility	7
2 Consumer Choice and Utility Maximization	19
3 Risk Attitude and Expected Utility	33
4 Production Maximization, Cost Minimization	49
5 Profit Maximization with Quadratic Equations	64
6 Monopoly, Monopolistic Competition, Oligopoly	75
7 Asymmetric Information	93

Introduction

Methods of Microeconomics applies mathematical methods to microeconomic topics to predict outcomes and calculate equilibrium values, and worked examples are combined with exercises and solutions for readers.

Consumer preferences and utility are examined with indifference curves, and differentiation to find marginal utility and the marginal rate of substitution. Consumer choice uses a Lagrange multiplier to perform constrained optimization of utility functions subject to a budget constraint. Risk attitude and expected utility look at absolute and relative risk aversion measures, and apply risk averse, neutral or risk loving attitudes to find the expected utility linked with gambling or buying insurance.

Production maximization optimizes production functions subject to cost constraints, and cost minimization optimizes cost functions subject to production constraints. Profit maximization with quadratic cost functions is performed for perfectly competitive or monopoly firms. Monopoly, monopolistically competitive, and oligopoly equilibrium values are calculated with optimization.

Finally, the effects of asymmetric information are examined by comparing actual, equilibrium, and efficient results for buyers and sellers.

1 Consumer Preferences and Utility

Mathematics can be used on a consumer's utility function to determine preferences, indifference curves, marginal utility and the marginal rate of substitution between goods.

EXAMPLE 1.1

A consumer's utility function is $U = 2x_1 + 4x_2$. U represents utility, x_1 represents the number of units of good 1, and x_2 represents the number of units of good 2. Find the consumer's indifference curves, preferences, their marginal utility and the marginal rate of substitution.

Answer 1.1

The first step to create an indifference curve is to create a hypothetical value for utility, U, and it can be simply denoted as a constant value, K. This gives $U = 2x_1 + 4x_2 = K$. The next step is to simplify and rearrange the equation in terms of x_1 or x_2 to show the relationship between the two goods. To write the utility equation in terms of x_1 both sides of the equation are divided by 2:

$$2x_1 + 4x_2 = K$$
$$x_1 + 2x_2 = 0.5K$$

Then $2x_2$ must be subtracted from both sides of the equation to write it in terms of x_1:

$$x_1 = 0.5K - 2x_2$$

This is the indifference curve, and the form of the equation above shows it is a straight line with a constant factor or vertical intercept of $0.5K$, and a slope of -2.

The negative slope means the two goods here, x_1 and x_2, are negatively correlated in the consumer's preferences, and as the consumer increases the quantity of one good they will reduce the quantity of the other. This means the two goods are substitutes, and the straight line with constant slope means they are perfect substitutes, as the consumer's marginal rate of substitution (MRS) between the goods will be constant at all consumption levels.

The marginal rate of substitution of good x_1 to good x_2 ($MRSx_1x_2$) gives consumer preferences on the proportions of good x_1 to good x_2, and $MRSx_1x_2$ represents how 1 unit of good x_1 is valued in terms of the number of units of good x_2. This can be found with the utility equation, $U = 2x_1 + 4x_2 = K$, as the marginal rate of substitution of good x_1 to x_2 equals the marginal utility of good x_1 (MUx_1) divided by the marginal utility of good x_2 (MUx_2):

$$MRS_{x_1 x_2} = MU_{x_1} / MU_{x_2}$$

As the marginal utility of good x_1 (MU_{x_1}) represents the change in overall utility resulting from a unit change in x_1, it can be found with the partial derivative of the overall utility equation (U) with respect to x_1, denoted as U_{x1}:

$$MU_{x_1} = U_{x1}$$

The derivative is the change, and the partial derivative of the utility function with respect to x_1 notes the effect of a unit change in x_1 on overall utility. A partial derivative is found by multiplying a variable's power by its coefficient, and then reducing the power by 1 (i.e. the 'power rule'):

$$U = 2x_1 + 4x_2$$
$$U_{x1} = (1)\, 2x_1^0$$
$$U_{x1} = MU_{x_1} = 2$$

Here the x_1 coefficient of 2 was multiplied by the x_1 power 1, before the power of 1 was reduced by 1 for an x_1 power of zero: x_1^0 (and an x value to the power of 0 equals 1). Putting these two together gives a coefficient of 2, multiplied by 1, for a result of 2 overall. And the same process can be used to find the marginal utility of good x_2, MU_{x_2}, which equals the partial derivative of the utility function with respect to x_2, U_{x2}:

$$MU_{x2} = U_{x2}$$

The method to find U_{x2} is the same as for x_1, except the partial differentiation is performed on x_2:

$$U = 2x_1 + 4x_2$$
$$U_{x2} = (1)\, 4x_2^0$$
$$U_{x2} = MU_{x2} = 4$$

The x_2 coefficient of 4 was multiplied by the x_2 power 1, before the power was reduced by 1 to give an x_2 power of zero: x_2^0 (which equals 1 as explained). Together this gives a coefficient of 4, multiplied by 1, for a result of 4 overall. With marginal utility values for both good x_1 and good x_2 the marginal rate of substitution can be found:

$$MRSx_1x_2 = MU_{x1} / MU_{x2}$$
$$MRSx_1x_2 = 2 / 4$$
$$MRSx_1x_2 = 0.5$$

The marginal rate of substitution of good x_1 to good x_2 is 0.5, and in order to gain 1 unit of x_1 the consumer would give up 0.5 units of x_2. This implies (by multiplying both these values by two) that in order to gain 1 unit of good x_2 the consumer would give up 2 units of good x_1. In simple terms one unit of good x_2 has twice the impact on utility as one unit of good x_1, and is therefore twice as popular.

EXAMPLE 1.2

A consumer's utility function is $U = \min\{2x_1, 3x_2\}$, where x_1 is the number of units of good x_1 and x_2 the number of units of good x_2. Determine the consumer's indifference curves, preferences, marginal utility, and their marginal rate of substitution.

Answer 1.2

The 'min' in the utility function stands for 'minimum', and utility here will either be determined by the value of $2x_1$ <u>or</u> that of $3x_2$, whichever is lower. The minimum in a utility equation signals that the goods are perfect complements, and to raise the utility of the consumer a minimum of both good x_1 and good x_2 is required.

With perfect complement goods the analysis is simple. The consumer prefers to consume the goods together or not at all, and consumption of only one good does not add to marginal utility. This means there is no marginal utility values to calculate for each good. It also means there can be no substitution between the goods at all, and therefore no marginal rate of substitution. Without a marginal rate of substitution indifference curves will not have slopes here, but instead are vertical lines (a zero slope on the horizontal axis) and horizontal lines (a zero slope on vertical axis), with the two line types joined by a right angle facing north-east in a diagram. This right angle where lines meet is the point of interest with perfect complement goods, and it is found by switching the coefficients of goods x_1 and x_2.

Utility function $U = \min\{2x_1, 3x_2\}$ gives indifference curve right angles at $3x_1$ and $2x_2$, and the consumer's preferences sees the goods consumed in a proportion of 3 units of good x_1 to 2 units of good x_2. This keeps both goods in balance in the utility equation as perfect complements require (i.e. $2(3) = 3(2)$).

EXAMPLE 1.3

A consumer's utility function is $U = x_1^{0.3} x_2^{0.5}$. Find the consumer's indifference curves and preferences, marginal utility, and their marginal rate of substitution.

Answer 1.3

The two goods here are neither perfect substitutes nor perfect complements but somewhere in the middle. As the goods exhibit some substitutability an indifference curve can be created using the same method as noted in example 1.1 for perfect substitutes, and by simplifying the utility equation so the goods can be written in terms of the other.

It will be simpler to present the indifference curve in terms of x_2 instead of x_1 here, as the 0.5 power term (same as square root, $\sqrt{}$) is easier to deal with than a 0.3 power term. The first step to simplify the utility equation so good x_2 is written in terms of good x_1 is to give the utility equation a constant value, K. This creates U: $x_1^{0.3} x_2^{0.5} = K$. Next both sides of the equation must be divided by $x_1^{0.3}$ to get the $x_2^{0.5}$ variable alone on one side:

$$x_1^{0.3} x_2^{0.5} = K$$
$$x_2^{0.5} = K / x_1^{0.3}$$

Then both sides should be squared to leave one unit of x_2 alone by itself (as $x_2^{0.5}$ equals $\sqrt{x_2}$):

$$x_2 = (K / x_1^{0.3})^2$$

This is the indifference curve, and it shows how the consumer values good x_2 in terms of good x_1. Here the indifference curve will actually be a curve. It won't be a straight line due to the absence of a separate intercept term (all straight lines cross an axis at some point for an intercept), nor two lines joined at a right angle as goods can be written in terms of each other and are substitutable.

The marginal rate of substitution of good x_1 to good x_2 ($MRSx_1x_2$) is found in the same way as example 1, by dividing the marginal utility of good x_1 by that of good x_2, $MRSx_1x_2 = MUx_1 / MUx_2$. And these marginal utilities are found using partial differentiation of the utility function with respect to good x_1 and then with respect to good x_2.

$$U = x_1^{0.3}x_2^{0.5}$$
$$U_{x1} = 0.3x_1^{-0.7}x_2^{0.5}$$
$$\text{Therefore } MUx_1 = 0.3x_1^{-0.7}x_2^{0.5}$$

Here the power of good x_1 (0.3) was multiplied by good x_1's coefficient (1), before the power was reduced by 1 (from 0.3 to -0.7). This gives $0.3x_1^{-0.7}$ which is combined with the unchanged other part of the utility equation (i.e. using the 'product rule'), for a result of $0.3x_1^{-0.7}x_2^{0.5}$.

Next partial differentiation occurs for x_2, and the 0.5 power becomes the coefficient, before the power falls by 1 to become -0.5. The x_1 part of the equation is unchanged.

$$U = x_1^{0.3}x_2^{0.5}$$
$$U_{x2} = x_1^{0.3}0.5x_2^{-0.5}$$
$$\text{Therefore } MUx_2 = x_1^{0.3}0.5x_2^{-0.5}$$

The marginal rate of substitution (MRS) divides one marginal utility value by the other, and simplifies the two equations. This simplification uses the mathematical principle that a variable can be moved from the top of a fraction to the bottom, or vice versa, if the sign of its power is changed (i.e. positive power to negative power, or negative to positive). For example, $2^4 / 1 = 1 / 2^{-4}$, and $2^{-4} / 1 = 1 / 2^4$. With this rule in mind, and the rule that multiplying a factor by itself results in their powers being added together (e.g. x^2 multiplied by $x^3 = x^5$), the MRS is:

$$MRS_{x_1x_2} = MU_{x_1} / MU_{x_2}$$
$$MRS_{x_1x_2} = 0.3x_1^{-0.7}x_2^{0.5} / x_1^{0.3}0.5x_2^{-0.5}$$
$$MRS_{x_1x_2} = (0.3) x_2^{0.5+0.5} / x_1^{0.3+0.7} (0.5)$$
$$MRS_{x_1x_2} = (0.3) x_2 / x_1 (0.5)$$
$$MRS_{x_1x_2} = 0.6 x_2 / x_1$$

The marginal rate of substitution (MRS) of good x_1 to good x_2 is $0.6 x_2 / x_1$, and one unit of good x_1 will be exchanged for this amount of good x_2. This reveals that the marginal rate of substitution isn't a constant value, and as x_2 increases or x_1 decreases the MRS will increase, while if the value of the x_2 decreases or x_1 increases the MRS will decrease.

EXERCISES 1

To test understanding of the topic of consumer preferences and utility readers can attempt to answer the following exercise questions, and the methods and solutions to the exercises are presented afterwards.

Calculate indifferences curves, marginal utility, and the marginal rate of substitution for these utility functions:

1. *U = 5x$_1$ + 4x$_2$*
2. *U = min{3x$_1$, 47x$_2$}*
3. *U = x$_1^2$x$_2^2$*

SOLUTIONS 1

1. $U = 5x_1 + 4x_2$

First set the utility function equal to a constant value, K. Next, subtract $4x_2$ from both sides to separate goods x_1 and x_2. Then divide both sides of the equation by 5 to present it in terms of x_1 to give the indifference curve:

$$5x_1 + 4x_2 = K$$
$$5x_1 = K - 4x_2$$
$$x_1 = K/5 - 0.8x_2$$

The indifference curve is a straight line, with intercept of K/5 and a constant slope of –0.8, and represents perfect substitute goods. The marginal utility of good x_1, MUx_1, and of x_2, MUx_2, is found with partial differentiation of the utility function. Dividing the former marginal utility by the latter gives the marginal rate of substitution, $MRSx_1x_2$:

$$U = 5x_1 + 4x_2$$
$$U_{x1} = MUx_1 = 5$$
$$U_{x2} = MUx_2 = 4$$

$$MRSx_1x_2 = MUx_1 / MUx_2$$
$$MRSx_1x_2 = 5 / 4$$
$$MRSx_1x_2 = 1.25$$

The marginal rate of substitution is constant at 1.25, and the consumer would exchange 1 unit of good x_1 for 1.25 units of good x_2.

2. $U = min\{3x_1, 47x_2\}$

The min (minimum) term reveals the goods to be perfect complements, and indifference curves will be vertical and horizontal lines joined by a right angle.

The right angles of the indifference curves will be at $47x_1$ and $3x_2$, and the coefficients of the two goods in the utility equation are simply switched to keep the two goods in balance (i.e. $3(47) = 47(3)$).

There aren't marginal utility values nor a marginal rate of substitution with perfect complements, as there is a zero slope and substitution between the goods isn't possible.

3. $U = x_1^2 x_2^2$

First set the utility function equal to a constant value, K. Then divide both sides of the equation by x_2^2 to get the x_1 variable on a separate side. Finally take the square root of everything to give x_1 and present the indifference curve:

$$x_1^2 x_2^2 = K$$
$$x_1^2 = K/x_2^2$$
$$x_1 = \sqrt{K}/x_2$$

This indifference curve is a curve, not a straight line as there is no separate intercept term, and not two lines joined by a right angle as substitutability exists between goods.

The marginal rate of substitution between goods x_1 and x_2 ($MRSx_1x_2$) divides the x_1 marginal utility (MUx_1) by that for x_2 (MUx_2). Marginal utility is found with partial differentiation, and this multiplies the coefficient of a variable by its power, then reduces the power by 1:

$$U = x_1^2 x_2^2$$
$$U_{x1} = MUx_1 = 2x_1 x_2^2$$
$$U_{x2} = MUx_2 = x_1^2 2x_2$$

$$MRSx_1x_2 = MUx_1 / MUx_2$$
$$MRSx_1x_2 = 2x_1 x_2^2 / x_1^2 2x_2$$

And this can be simplified down by removing factors which are common to both the top and bottom of the fraction, and this action removes an x_1, x_2 and a (2):

$$MRSx_1x_2 = x_2 / x_1$$

The marginal rate of substitution (MRS) is x_2 / x_1, and one unit of good x_1 will be exchanged for this amount of good x_2. This MRS is not constant, and it will increase as x_2 increases in value or x_1 decreases, while the MRS will decrease as x_2 decreases in value or x_1 increases.

2 Consumer Choice and Utility Maximization

Consumer choice and utility maximization can be calculated by combining a consumer's utility function with their budget constraint. The maximization process involves constrained optimization and a Lagrange multiplier.

EXAMPLE 2.1

A consumer's utility function is $U = 2x_1 3x_2$, and the consumer naturally seeks to optimize this function by selecting the quantities of good x_1 and good x_2 which can offer them the maximum utility possible. However, the consumer's attempted optimization will be constrained by their budget and they only have £30 to spend, while good x_1 costs £3 per unit to buy, and good x_2 costs £2 per unit to buy. Using all of this information derive the quantities of goods x_1 and x_2 which the consumer will choose.

Answer 2.1

The consumer here seeks to maximize utility function $U = 2x_1 3x_2$, subject to a budget constraint which can be denoted as $p_1x_1 + p_2x_2 = M$. In this constraint x_1 and x_2 are the quantities of good 1 and 2 respectively, p_1 (£3) and p_2 (£2) are the prices of good 1 and 2 respectively, and M is their money budget (£30). The budget constraint sees the total of the consumer's expenditure (price of good 1 multiplied by the quantity of good 1, added to price of good 2 multiplied by quantity of good 2) as equal (=) to the money budget (M), not greater or less than it. Total expenditure naturally can't exceed the consumer's budget, and total expenditure won't be less than the consumer's complete budget as they are thought to put all of their available budget to the goal of maximizing their utility.

For this example to be solved a Lagrange multiplier (L) must be set up, and this involves writing the utility function and the budget constraint together as one equation to be maximized. There are three parts to this and first the prices of goods x_1 and x_2, $p_1 = £3$ and $p_2 = £2$, must be inserted into the budget constraint equation along with the consumer's budget of $M = £30$, to give $3x_1 + 2x_2 = 30$. Second, this budget constraint must be rearranged so that M and the price multiplied by quantity terms are on the same side, and this simply involves subtracting the price by quantity terms from both sides: $30 - 3x_1 - 2x_2$. Third and finally a new variable, the Greek letter lambda (λ), must be multiplied by the budget constraint variables to denote their separate role, in preparation for partial differentiation. The result of these three steps is as follows:

$$L = 2x_1 3x_2 + \lambda[30 - 3x_1 - 2x_2]$$

This Lagrange multiplier (L) is an equation ready to maximize consumer utility given their budget constraint and the goods' prices. It will be maximized at a point and level of consumption where marginal utility (i.e. the change in utility, the effect of the last unit of a good, called the derivative and found using differentiation) equals zero. Positive marginal utility means utility is increasing and isn't yet maximized, while negative marginal utility means utility is declining, but zero marginal utility means utility is changing direction and therefore at its maximum. While it could in theory also mean utility is at its minimum the form of the Lagrange multiplier will prevent this.

There are three factors to the Lagrange multiplier, good x_1, good x_2, and lambda λ which separates the budget constraint from the goods. And as each factor has a different relationship with utility they must be differentiated individually, using partial differentiation. In the following terms L_{x1} represents partial differentiation of the Lagrange multiplier with respect to good x_1, L_{x2} represents partial differentiation of the Lagrange multiplier with respect to good x_2, and L_λ represents partial differentiation of the Lagrange multiplier with respect to the budget constraint factors. And these terms are turned into three separate equations and set equal to zero, to give the scenarios where the consumer has maximum utility:

$$L = 2x_1 3x_2 + \lambda[30 - 3x_1 - 2x_2]$$
$$\underline{\text{Equation 1}}: L_{x_1} = (2)3x_2 - 3\lambda = 0$$
$$\underline{\text{Equation 2}}: L_{x_2} = 2x_1(3) - 2\lambda = 0$$
$$\underline{\text{Equation 3}}: L_\lambda = 30 - 3x_1 - 2x_2 = 0$$

These partial derivatives then have to be rearranged to find the individual values of x_1 and x_2 which give maximum utility. This can be done using the lambda term, λ, and equations 1 and 2:

$$\underline{\text{Equation 1}}: (2)3x_2 - 3\lambda = 0$$
$$6x_2 = 3\lambda$$
$$\lambda = 2x_2$$

$$\underline{\text{Equation 2}}: 2x_1(3) - 2\lambda = 0$$
$$6x_1 = 2\lambda$$
$$\lambda = 3x_1$$

Combining the two results for λ reveals that $\lambda = 3x_1 = 2x_2$. Therefore $x_1 = 2/3\ x_2$. This relationship between good x_1 and good x_2 may be referred to as equation 4:

$$\underline{\text{Equation 4}}: x_1 = 2/3\ x_2.$$

Next equation 4 is substituted into equation 3, the budget constraint, to create a new equation known as equation 5 which reveals the precise value of good x_2:

Equation 3: $30 - 3x_1 - 2x_2 = 0$

$$30 - 3(2/3\ x_2) - 2x_2 = 0$$
$$30 - 2x_2 - 2x_2 = 0$$
$$30 = 4x_2$$
Equation 5: $x_2 = 7.5$

Finally, equation 5 is substituted into equation 3 to give the value of x_1, which can be known as equation 6:

$$30 - 3x_1 - 2(7.5) = 0$$
$$30 = 3x_1 + 15$$
$$15 = 3x_1$$
Equation 6: $x_1 = 5$

The consumer here achieves maximum utility with $x_1 = 5$ units and $x_2 = 7.5$ units. The associated level of utility is calculated by putting these values into the utility function, $U = 2x_1 3x_2$, for $U = 2(5)3(7.5) = 225$. And these values are confirmed as possible when entered into the budget constraint, $p_1 x_1 + p_2 x_2 = M$, for $3(5) + 2(7.5) = 30$.

The procedure to find the utility maximizing values of goods can be summarized and remembered with six separate equations. Equations 1, 2 and 3 give the partial derivative of the Lagrange multiplier with respect to x_1, x_2 and λ respectively. Equation 4 uses equations 1 and 2 and λ to find the relationship between goods x_1 and x_2;

equation 5 combines equations 3 and 4 to reveal the value of x_2; and equation 6 combines equations 3 and 5 to calculate the value of x_1.

EXAMPLE 2.2

A consumer's utility function is $U = x_1^2 + 2x_2^2$, their budget is £36, the price of good x_1 is £2 per unit, and the price of good x_2 is £2 per unit. Determine the levels of x_1 and x_2 which offer the consumer the maximum utility.

Answer 2.2

Before any analysis is undertaken the first thing to note is that the goods here are perfect substitutes, as shown by the utility function where good x_1 and x_2 are added to each other, instead of being multiplied by each other as in example 2.1. With perfect substitutes there is the possibility that the consumer could only consume one of the two goods and have zero units of the second good, a situation known as a 'corner solution'. If this were the case then the utility function and budget constraint would only contain the one good, and therefore it's worth ensuring that this situation doesn't occur here.

Proceeding with the original utility maximization process when one of the goods actually has a zero value will give an incorrect result, as it enforces the idea that both goods have a non-zero value when they don't. This may lead to utility minimization and not maximization. It is possible to assess if utility minimization has occurred by looking at the sign of the second derivative of the Lagrange function (positive sign means minimization, negative sign means maximization), but to save time it's worth determining if one of the goods won't be consumed at all before running through the Lagrange method.

In the utility function here, $x_1^2 + 2x_2^2$, the coefficient of good x_2 is twice that of good x_1 (i.e. 2 to 1), and good x_2 has a greater effect on utility than good x_1. The consumer here would therefore be tempted to only consume good x_2, which is possible as the goods are perfect substitutes, and the only thing that would stop them is if the price of good x_2 was significantly more than that of good x_1 so that utility and prices balanced out. However, with good x_1 priced at £2 per unit and good x_2 also priced at £2 per unit the prices and utility don't balance out. The consumer will therefore only select to consume good x_2 and will select zero units of good x_1. With zero units of x_1 the good and its price (p_1) are now irrelevant to the utility maximization problem, and they can be removed. This gives a new utility function to be maximized of $U = 2x_2^2$, and the budget of $M = £36$ and price of good x_2 at $p_2 = £2$ per unit gives a new budget constraint of $p_2 x_2 = M$, and $2x_2 = 36$.

As noted in the last example the first step is to set up the Lagrange multiplier (L), and this takes the form $L =$

'utility function' + λ['rearranged budget constraint']. The utility function is 'U = $2x_2^2$', and the rearranged budget constraint (p_2x_2 = M is rearranged to become 'M – p_2x_2') is '36 – $2x_2$'. This gives the following Lagrange multiplier:

$$L = 2x_2^2 + \lambda[36 - 2x_2]$$

Next the Lagrange multiplier (L) is differentiated with respect to good x_2 and λ, as good x_1 is now irrelevant, to create two new equations which are all put equal to zero:

$$L_{x2} = 4x_2 - 2\lambda = 0$$
$$L_\lambda = 36 - 2x_2 = 0$$

The second equation can then simply be rearranged to find the number of units of good x_2 which the consumer will select:

$$L_\lambda = 36 - 2x_2 = 0$$
$$36 = 2x_2$$
$$x_2 = 18$$

The consumer therefore achieves maximum utility with consumption levels of x_1 = 0 units and x_2 = 18 units. The associated level of utility is calculated by putting these values into the original utility function, U = $x_1^2 + 2x_2^2$, for U = $(0)^2 + 2(18)^2$ = 648. And these values are confirmed as possible when entered into the original budget constraint, $p_1x_1 + p_2x_2 = M$, for $2(0) + 2(18) = 36$. In practice of course the Lagrange multiplier method wasn't required here, and once it was deduced that only one of the two goods would be consumed the money budget could have simply been divided by that good's price. This would also give the result £36 / 2 = 18 units of good x_1. But it's worth running through the Lagrange process as practice and to confirm that it gives the same result.

EXERCISES 2

To test understanding of the topic of consumer choice and utility maximization readers can attempt to answer the following exercise questions, and the methods and solutions to the exercises are presented afterwards.

Calculate the levels of x_1 and x_2 which maximize a consumer's utility levels given the following utility functions, and the corresponding goods prices and budget:

1. $U = x_1^2 x_2$, where good x_1 costs £4 per unit, good x_2 costs £6 per unit, and the budget is £54.

2. $U = 3x_1^2 + 3x_2^2$, where good x_1 costs £2 per unit, good x_2 costs £3 per unit, and the consumer's money budget is £50.

SOLUTIONS 2

1. $U = x_1^2 x_2$. $p_1 = 4$. $p_2 = 6$. $M = 54$

First set up the Lagrange multiplier:

$$L = x_1^2 x_2 + \lambda[54 - 4x_1 - 6x_2]$$

Next create equations 1, 2 and 3 by partial differentiation with respect to goods x_1, x_2 and λ respectively:

<u>Equation 1</u>: $L_{x1} = 2x_1 x_2 - 4\lambda = 0$
<u>Equation 2</u>: $L_{x2} = x_1^2 - 6\lambda = 0$
<u>Equation 3</u>: $L_\lambda = 54 - 4x_1 - 6x_2 = 0$

And equations 1 and 2, and the value of λ, can be used to find the relationship between goods x_1 and x_2:

<u>Equation 1</u>: $2x_1 x_2 - 4\lambda = 0$
$2x_1 x_2 = 4\lambda$
$\lambda = 0.5 x_1 x_2$

<u>Equation 2</u>: $x_1^2 - 6\lambda = 0$
$x_1^2 = 6\lambda$
$\lambda = (1/6) x_1^2$

This reveals that $\lambda = 0.5x_1x_2 = (1/6)x_1^2$, but unfortunately this isn't enough to find a relationship between good x_1 and good x_2, as both terms have an x_1 in them which prevents one good from being seen in terms of the other. However, this can easily be resolved by first dividing everything by x_1:

$$\lambda/x_1 = 0.5x_2 = (1/6)x_1$$

And then multiplying everything by 6 to reveal the relationship between the two goods in terms of one unit of good x_1, to be known as equation 4:

$$(6)\lambda/x_1 = 3x_2 = x_1$$

Equation 4: $x_1 = 3x_2$

Equation 4 can then be substituted into equation 3 to reveal the value of good x_2, which is equation 5:

Equation 3: $54 - 4x_1 - 6x_2 = 0$

$$54 - 4(3x_2) - 6x_2 = 0$$
$$54 - 12x_2 - 6x_2 = 0$$
$$54 - 18x_2 = 0$$
$$54 = 18x_2$$
Equation 5: $x_2 = 3$

And then equation 5 can be substituted into equation 3 to reveal the value of good x_1, known as equation 6:

$$54 - 4x_1 - 6(3) = 0$$
$$54 - 4x_1 - 18 = 0$$
$$36 - 4x_1 = 0$$
$$36 = 4x_1$$
Equation 6: $x_1 = 9$

Consumer utility is maximized with $x_1 = 9$ and $x_2 = 3$. The associated level of utility is calculated by putting these values into the utility function, $U = x_1^2 x_2$, for $U = (9)^2(3) = 243$. And these values are confirmed as possible when entered into the budget constraint, $p_1 x_1 + p_2 x_2 = M$, for $4(9) + 6(3) = 54$.

2. $U = 3x_1^2 + 3x_2^2$. $p_1 = 2$. $p_2 = 3$. $M = 50$

The first thing to note is that the goods here are perfect substitutes, as shown by the utility function taking the form where the utility for good x_1 and the utility for good x_2 are added to each other, $U = 3x_1^2 + 3x_2^2$, instead of being multiplied by each other as in the last exercise. This form of utility function opens up the possibility for a 'corner solution' where the consumption level of one of the two goods could be zero, and the consumer only chooses to have one good as it offers more than the other good relative to its price. Each good's individual utility relative to its price will determine if the consumer decides to only consume one good.

In this example good x_1 and good x_2 both have the same relationship with utility, and both have a coefficient of 3 and a power of 2. Therefore one unit of either of the two goods will have exactly the same impact on utility as the other good, and the prices of the two goods would be expected to be the same as a result. However, this is not the case in this example, and good x_1 has a price of £2 per unit while good x_2 has a higher price of £3 per unit. There is no reason for the consumer to pay more for good x_2 when good x_1 offers the same utility per unit at a lower price, and therefore the consumer can be expected to take advantage of the perfect substitute nature of the two goods to only consume good x_1, for a corner solution to the consumer choice question.

With the consumer having zero units of good x_2 that good and its now irrelevant price can be eliminated from the analysis completely, and the original utility function and budget constraint can be simplified to the following utility function, good price and budget: $U = 3x_1^2$, $p_1 = 2$, $M = 50$. Using these values gives a Lagrange multiplier as follows:

$$L = 3x_1^2 + \lambda[50 - 2x_1]$$

And this Lagrange only has to be partially differentiated with respect to good x_1 and λ, as there is no good x_2 here:

$$L_{x1} = 6x_1 - 2\lambda = 0$$
$$L_\lambda = 50 - 2x_1 = 0$$

The second equation here, L_λ, can then be rearranged to give the value of x_1 which offers maximum utility without any need for further analysis:

$$50 - 2x_1 = 0$$
$$50 = 2x_1$$
$$x_1 = 25$$

The consumer here will maximize utility with $x_1 = 25$ units, and $x_2 = 0$ units. The associated level of utility is calculated by putting these values into the utility function, $U = 3x_1^2 + 3x_2^2$, for $U = 3(25)^2 + 3(0)^2 = 1{,}875$. And these values are confirmed as possible when entered into the budget constraint, $p_1x_1 + p_2x_2 = M$, for $2(25) + 3(0) = 50$.

3 Risk Attitude and Expected Utility

A consumer's utility function can be used to find their risk attitude and level of absolute or relative risk aversion. Utility can also be combined with expected probabilities to create expected utility theory, and this method can determine if a consumer will proceed with a gamble, or calculate the most a consumer will pay for insurance and how much of this is a risk premium paid to avoid risk.

EXAMPLE 3.1

Consumer 1 has the utility function $U = \sqrt{W}$ and consumer 2 has the utility function $U = W^2$, where W represents the level of wealth. Using these utility functions answer the following questions:

(i) Determine each consumer's risk attitude and explain if they are risk averse, risk neutral, or risk loving;

(ii) Calculate the Arrow-Pratt values for absolute and relative risk aversion for each consumer;

(iii) Imagine that the original level of wealth for each consumer was £25 and they each had to choose whether to risk £9 in a gamble for a chance of a £100 return (made up by a £91 prize and a return of the £9 stake). Determine if either consumer would proceed with the gamble when the probabilities of winning were judged to be 0.1, or 0.5.

Answer 3.1

(i) An individual's risk attitude is determined by the relationship between wealth and their utility. A risk averse individual wants to hold on to what they have and not risk it for a chance of greater wealth, and a wealth increase will be associated with a smaller increase in utility in relative terms. A risk loving individual is willing to put their current wealth at risk for a chance of more wealth, and a wealth increase will be associated with a greater increase in utility in relative terms. And a risk neutral person has no preference either way, and a wealth increase will be matched by the same relative increase in utility.

Taking the second derivative of the utility function (i.e. derivative of the derivative, change of the change) can show the relationship between wealth and utility and an individual's risk attitude, by showing the relative growth in utility as wealth rises. A risk averse person's utility function has a negative second derivative (i.e. diminishing utility growth), a risk lover has a utility function with a positive second derivative (i.e. increasing utility growth), and a risk neutral person has a utility function without a second derivative (i.e. no change, constant utility growth).

Consumer 1 has a utility function of $U = \sqrt{W}$, which is the same as $U = W^{0.5}$, and this means that a wealth increase will result in a far smaller increase in utility. The first derivative of this function is $U' = 0.5W^{-0.5}$, and the second derivative is $U'' = -0.25W^{-1.5}$. As the second derivative is negative consumer 1 is risk averse.

Consumer 2 has a utility function of $U = W^2$, which means that a wealth increase will result in a far greater increase in utility. The first derivative of this function is $U' = 2W$, and the second derivative is $U'' = 2$. As the second derivative is positive consumer 2 is risk loving.

(ii) Absolute and relative risk aversion can be represented using the Arrow-Pratt measures, where an individual's absolute risk aversion equals the negative of the second derivative of the utility function, $-U''$, divided by the first derivative of the utility function, U':

$$\text{Absolute Risk Aversion} = -U'' / U'$$

An individual's relative risk aversion is simply their absolute risk aversion multiplied by their level of wealth:

$$\text{Relative Risk Aversion} = (W) -U'' / U'$$

The first derivative of consumer 1's utility function has already been calculated at $U' = 0.5W^{-0.5}$, and the second derivative of their utility function has already been calculated at $U'' = -0.25W^{-1.5}$. The absolute risk aversion (ARA) of consumer 1, $-U''/U'$, is therefore:

$$ARA = -U''/U'$$
$$ARA = (-) -0.25W^{-1.5} / 0.5W^{-0.5}$$
$$ARA = 0.5\ W^{-1.5} / W^{-0.5}$$
$$ARA = (0.5)\ 1 / W^{-0.5+1.5}$$
$$ARA = (0.5)\ 1 / W$$
$$ARA = 0.5 / W$$

And the relative risk aversion (RRA) of consumer 1 is simply this multiplied by wealth:

$$RRA = (W) -U''/U'$$
$$RRA = (W)\ 0.5 / W$$
$$RRA = 0.5$$

The first derivative of consumer 1's utility function is $U' = 2W$, and the second derivative is $U'' = 2$. This gives an ARA for consumer 2 at:

$$ARA = -2/2W$$
$$ARA = -1/W$$

And consumer 2's RRA is this value multiplied by W:

$$RRA = -1$$

(iii) This question uses expected utility theory, which combines a utility function with probabilities of occurrence to determine the utility derived from various options. For example, while consumer 1's utility function is $U = \sqrt{W}$ their expected utility, $E(U)$, is $E(U) = P*\sqrt{W}$, where P is the probability of a certain level of wealth occurring (P is probability not price with expected utility).

First the situation with a 0.1 probability (i.e. a 10% chance) of winning the gamble will be examined. If consumer 1 wins the gamble they get £100 wealth (W_1, the £9 stake and £91 prize), and there is a 0.1 probability, P, of this happening. That leaves a 0.9 (i.e. 90%), 1 − P, probability that they lose the bet and end up with £16 (W_2, the original wealth of £25, minus lost £9 stake). This gives the following equation for expected wealth:

$$\text{Expected wealth} = 0.1\,(100) + 0.9\,(16)$$

However, this equation doesn't account for consumer 1's risk attitude, and their utility function ($U = \sqrt{W}$) must be added to the analysis to create an expected utility, $E(U)$, equation to reveal what they gain from taking the gamble:

$$E(U) = P(\sqrt{W_1}) + (1 - P)(\sqrt{W_2})$$
$$E(U) = 0.1\,(\sqrt{100}) + 0.9\,(\sqrt{16})$$
$$E(U) = 0.1(10) + 0.9(4)$$
$$E(U) = 4.6$$

If consumer 1 goes ahead with the gamble with odds of winning at 0.1 they gain an expected utility of 4.6. This can be compared with what they stand to gain if they don't gamble and just keep the £25 they hold in initial wealth:

$$E(U) = \sqrt{(W)}$$
$$E(U) = \sqrt{25}$$
$$E(U) = 5$$

If consumer 1 doesn't gamble then they gain expected utility of 5, which exceeds the expected utility gain of 4.6 when the probability of winning is 0.1. Therefore consumer 1 is better off not gambling with these odds of success, and they can be expected to avoid the gamble.

The expected utility method can then be applied to consumer 2, who faces the same wealth opportunities and odds as consumer 1 but has a different utility function, $U = W^2$. With a 0.1 probability of winning the gamble the expected utility of the gamble for consumer 2 is:

$$E(U) = 0.1\,(100^2) + 0.9\,(16^2)$$
$$E(U) = 0.1\,(10{,}000) + 0.9\,(256)$$
$$E(U) = 1{,}000 + 230.4$$
$$E(U) = 1{,}230.4$$

Consumer 2 gains expected utility of 1,230.4 if they take the gamble, and this must be compared to their utility if they don't take the gamble to see if they will proceed with it. The wealth associated with not taking the gamble is the original wealth of 25, and combining this with consumer 2's utility function $U = W^2$ gives:

$$E(U) = W^2$$
$$E(U) = 25^2$$
$$E(U) = 625$$

If consumer 2 doesn't gamble they gain an expected utility of 625 from their wealth level, lower than the expected utility of 1,230.4 associated with taking the gamble when the probability of winning is 0.1. Therefore it is in consumer 2's best interests to gamble and this is what they would be expected to do.

Turning next to the scenario where the probability of winning the gamble is 0.5 (i.e. 50%), the wealth associated with not taking the gamble is the same as before at £25, and consumer 1 again gains expected utility of 5 from this while consumer 2 gains expected utility of 625. However, the expected wealth function associated with taking the gamble changes to the following with the 0.5 probability:

Expected wealth = 0.5 (100) + 0.5 (16)

And this gives an expected utility function for consumer 1 at:

$$E(U) = 0.5\ (\sqrt{100}) + 0.5\ (\sqrt{16})$$
$$E(U) = 0.5(10) + 0.5(4)$$
$$E(U) = 7$$

Consumer 1 gains expected utility of 7 from taking the gamble if the probability of winning is 0.5, and as this exceeds the expected utility of 5 they gain from not taking the gamble consumer 1 can be expected to gamble.

With a win probability of 0.5 consumer 2's expected utility becomes:

$$E(U) = 0.5\ (100^2) + 0.5\ (16^2)$$
$$E(U) = 0.5\ (10,000) + 0.5\ (256)$$
$$E(U) = 5,000 + 128$$
$$E(U) = 5,128$$

The 5,128 expected utility consumer 2 gains from gambling exceeds the 1,230.4 expected utility they receive from not gambling, and therefore consumer 2 will gamble. Overall, risk loving consumer 2 gambles if the probability of winning is 0.1 or 0.5, while risk averse consumer 1 only gambles if the probability of winning is 0.5, not if it is 0.1.

EXAMPLE 3.2

A collection of individuals each hold assets worth £100 and all have the utility function $U = \sqrt{W}$. Some of the individuals have a 50% chance of losing £75, and they can be defined as group 1, while the remaining individuals have a 10% probability of losing the same amount of £75, and they can be known as group 2. Each individual knows which of the two groups they belong to and knows their own probability of a £75 loss. Using all of this information answer the following questions:

(i) What is the most each of the two groups would pay as an insurance premium to fully cover the risk of loss?

(ii) What is an actuarially fair premium for each of the two groups? And what is each group's risk premium?

(iii) Imagine that groups 1 and 2 are of equal size, and consider the consequences if an insurer can't differentiate between the two groups and must instead consider them as a single group with a probability of loss at 30%, the average of the two groups.

Answer 3.2

(i) Group 1 starts with wealth of £100, and if they don't take out an insurance premium they have a 50% probability of a £75 loss, which means a 50% chance of ending up with £25. They also have a 50% chance of losing nothing, which gives a 50% chance of £100. This gives the following expected wealth function:

Expected wealth = 0.5 (25) + 0.5 (100)

Adding utility, $U = \sqrt{W}$, gives expected utility:

$$E(U) = 0.5\,(\sqrt{25}) + 0.5\,(\sqrt{100})$$
$$E(U) = 0.5\,(5) + 0.5\,(10)$$
$$E(U) = 7.5$$

Not taking out insurance would leave individuals in group 1 (50% probability of a £75 loss) with expected utility of 7.5. Therefore group 1 will only get insurance if it leaves them with expected utility of at least 7.5, otherwise they will end up in a worse position. To find the wealth level which corresponds to utility of 7.5 the utility function for the individuals is simply reversed, and if utility is the square root of wealth, $U = \sqrt{W}$, then it follows that wealth equals utility squared, $W = U^2$:

$$W = U^2$$
$$W = 7.5^2$$
$$W = 56.25$$

Individuals in group 1 will be indifferent between the 50% risk of a £75 loss from their original wealth of £100, for expected utility of 7.5, and ending up with wealth of £56.25 after paying insurance to remove all risk of loss, which also gives 7.5 expected utility. Therefore the most individuals in group 1 would pay as an insurance premium to cover all risk of loss is £100 − £56.25 = £43.75.

Group 2 individuals only have a 10% risk of the £75 loss so their expected wealth function would be as follows, with a 0.1 probability of £25 and 0.9 probability of £100:

$$\text{Expected wealth} = 0.1\,(25) + 0.9\,(100)$$

Combining this expected wealth function with group 2's utility function, $U = \sqrt{W}$, gives the expected utility:

$$E(U) = 0.1\,(\sqrt{25}) + 0.9\,(\sqrt{100})$$
$$E(U) = 0.1\,(5) + 0.9\,(10)$$
$$E(U) = 0.5 + 9$$
$$E(U) = 9.5$$

And group 2 will be indifferent between taking the risk of a loss, for expected utility of 9.5, and paying a sum of money for insurance which left an amount of wealth which also gave expected utility of 9.5. This is again found with the inverse of the utility function, $U = \sqrt{W}$, $W = U^2$:

$$W = U^2$$
$$W = 9.5^2$$
$$W = 90.25$$

£100 – £90.25 = £9.75 is the most group 2 individuals would pay for insurance, and paying any more would leave them worse off than just taking the risk of the loss.

(ii) An actuarially fair premium (AFP) is simply the amount which is at risk of loss, multiplied by the probability of that loss. Both groups have £75 at risk, and group 1 has a probability of loss at 0.5, while group 2 has a probability of loss at 0.1. Therefore the AFP for group 1 = 75*0.5 = £37.50, and AFP for group 2 = 75*0.1 = £7.5.

The risk premium is the amount paid to avoid risk based on risk attitude, and it equals the difference between the most an individual would pay to avoid risk and the actuarially fair premium. The most group 1 individuals would pay for an insurance premium to fully cover risk is £43.75, and the group 1 AFP is £37.50, for a risk premium for group 1 of £43.75 − £37.50 = £6.25. The most group 2 individuals would pay for an insurance premium to fully cover risk is £9.75, and the AFP for group 2 is £7.50, for a risk premium of £9.75 − £7.50 = £2.25.

(iii) An insurer which can't determine the risk levels of individuals may charge an actuarially fair premium which averages the two groups' probabilities (0.1 and 0.5) for a 0.3 probability. Combining this probability with the £75 at risk gives 0.3*75 = £22.5 as the AFP. This amount is far higher than the most the low risk group 2 individuals would pay to avoid risk (£9.75), and far lower than the most the high risk group 1 individuals would pay to avoid risk (£43.75). Therefore the system is inefficient, and the low risk group won't get insurance but the high risk group will at an undercharged price, which will cost the insurer.

EXERCISES 3

To test understanding of the topic of risk attitude and expected utility readers can attempt to answer the following exercise questions, and the methods and solutions to the exercises are presented afterwards:

1. Consumer 1 has the utility function $U = 2W$, and consumer 2 has the utility function $U = 2W^2$.

(i) Is each consumer risk averse, risk neutral, or risk loving? What is their absolute and relative risk aversion?

(ii) Imagine each consumer had an initial wealth of £9, and was considering taking part in a gamble. Would either consumer be willing to gamble £5 for a chance to win a prize of £16 if the odds of winning were 20%?

2. A consumer has initial wealth of £150 and a utility function of $U = \sqrt{(2W)}$. They are considering buying a product priced at £100, but are unsure of its true value.

(i) The consumer thinks there is a 75% chance that the product is worth £200, and a 25% chance that it is worthless. Will the consumer buy the item?

(ii) Whether the consumer buys the item or not, what is the most they would pay to fully cover against a 25% risk of a £100 loss, and how much of this is a risk premium?

SOLUTIONS 3

1. (i) The second derivative of a consumer's utility function reveals their risk attitude. Consumer 1's utility function is $U = 2W$, and the first derivative is $U' = 2$, while the second derivative is $U'' = 0$. This result means that consumer 1 has a zero risk attitude, and they don't have a risk attitude at all. Therefore they are risk neutral. Consumer 2's utility function is $U = 2W^2$, and the first derivative of this is $U' = 4W$, while the second derivative of this is $U'' = 4$. This is a positive number which means that consumer 2 has a risk loving risk attitude.

Absolute risk aversion (ARA) = $-U''/U'$. For consumer 1 this gives ARA = $-0/2 = 0$. This is zero risk aversion, as consumer 1 is risk neutral. And consumer 1's relative risk aversion (RRA) is this result multiplied by wealth, W, which will again give a result of 0 for the same reason. For risk loving consumer 2 the ARA = $-4/4W = -1/W$, and their absolute risk aversion is negative not positive to show that they have the opposite of risk aversion. RRA is this result multiplied by W, RRA = -1.

1. (ii) If either consumer doesn't gamble they gain £9. If they do gamble they have a 0.8 probability of losing and ending up with £4 (i.e. £9 − £5 stake), and a 0.2 probability of winning and ending up with £21 (i.e. £16 prize + £5 stake returned). For consumer 1 with utility function $U = 2W$ the expected utility of each choice is:

$$\text{Don't gamble: } E(U) = 2(9)$$
$$E(U) = 18$$

$$\text{Gamble: } E(U) = 0.8\,[2(4)] + 0.2[2(21)]$$
$$E(U) = 6.4 + 8.4$$
$$E(U) = 14.8$$

As the expected utility for not gambling is 18 and this exceeds the 14.8 expected utility associated with taking the gamble risk neutral consumer 1 won't gamble.

Consumer 2 has utility function $U = 2W^2$ and the expected utility for the two possible choices are therefore:

$$\text{Don't gamble: } E(U) = 2(9^2)$$
$$E(U) = 162$$

$$\text{Gamble: } E(U) = 0.8\,[2(4^2)] + 0.2[2(21^2)]$$
$$E(U) = 25.6 + 176.4$$
$$E(U) = 202$$

Consumer 2 will gamble as it offers expected utility of 202, higher than the 162 associated with not gambling.

2. *(i)* If the consumer holds onto the 100 instead of spending it expected utility, $E(U) = \sqrt{(2W)} = \sqrt{(2*100)} = 14.142$. If they buy the item then the expected utility is:

$$E(U) = [0.75*\sqrt{(2*200)}] + [0.25*\sqrt{(2*0)}]$$

$$E(U) = 15 + 0$$
$$E(U) = 15$$

The expected utility from holding onto the £100 is 14.142, and this is less than the expected utility of 15 associated with spending the £100 on the item with uncertain value. Therefore the consumer will buy the item.

2. *(ii)* If there is a 25% chance of losing £100 there is, as no other information has been given here, a 75% chance of holding onto £100. The consumer's expected utility is:

$$E(U) = [0.75*\sqrt{(2*100)}] + [0.25*\sqrt{(2*0)}]$$
$$E(U) = 10.607$$

The consumer would be indifferent between taking the 25% risk of losing £100, for expected utility of 10.607, and paying some of the £100 as long as it left enough wealth to still offer expected utility of 10.607. The wealth corresponding to this expected utility can be found by reversing the utility function: $U = \sqrt{(2W)}$, $W = U^2/2$. $W = 10.607^2/2 = £56.25$. The consumer would pay £100 – £56.25 = £43.75 to fully cover the 25% risk of £100 loss.

The actuarially fair premium for a 25% chance of the £100 loss is 0.25*100 = £25. Taking this from £43.75, the most the consumer would pay to fully cover the risk, gives the risk premium a consumer pays based on their risk attitude: £43.75 – £25 = £18.75 risk premium.

4 Production Maximization, Cost Minimization

A producer's output can be maximized given cost constraints using constrained optimization and a Lagrange multiplier. And a producer's costs can be minimized given production resource constraints in a similar way.

EXAMPLE 4.1

A producer has the production function $Q = L^{0.2}K^{0.8}$, where Q is the quantity of units of output, L is labour inputs, and K is capital inputs. The producer seeks to maximize output quantity (Q) subject to a £500 cost constraint, with the price of labour given by the wage rate per hour, w = £9, and the price of capital given by its rental rate per hour, r = £40. Using this information determine the levels of labour and capital which maximize output, and calculate the maximum possible output.

Answer 4.1

The process for output maximization given a cost constraint is essentially the same as for utility maximization in the consumer choice section earlier, except output replaces utility, a cost constraint replaces a budget constraint, and the prices of labour and capital replace the prices of different goods to consume. Output maximization combines the production function to be maximized with the cost constraint using a Lagrange multiplier (*L*), *L* = 'production function' + λ['rearranged cost constraint']. The Lagrange multiplier is represented by an italic *L*, while labour is denoted with a non-italic L to make a distinction between the two.

Note that the production function here is a Cobb-Douglas production function, where the input factors (labour and capital) are combined and multiplied by each other. This removes the possibility for a corner solution where one of the variables equals zero, as it's not possible for one variable to equal zero without forcing the same effect on the other to prevent any output from being produced. The production function has already been given above, $Q = L^{0.2}K^{0.8}$, and the cost constraint, C, is equal to the quantity of labour (L) at its wage rate (w), wL, added to the quantity of capital (K) at its rental rate (r), rK: Cost constraint, C = wL + rK. In this example the cost constraint, C, is 500 = 9L + 40K. The Lagrange multiplier requires for this to be rearranged so it is all on one side without an equals sign, and rearranged cost constraint, C is 500 − 9L − 40K. The Lagrange multiplier is as follows:

$$L = L^{0.2}K^{0.8} + \lambda[500 - 9L - 40K]$$

And the three different variables here (L, K, and λ) are partially differentially separately to show the change in each, and then the result is put equal to zero to optimize (i.e. maximize here) it. As explained earlier differentiation involves multiplying a variable's coefficient by the variable's power, and then reducing the variable's power by 1. This creates three equations for future reference, where equation 1 is the partial derivative of the Lagrange multiplier with respect to labour, L_L, equation 2 is the partial derivative of the Lagrange multiplier with respect to capital, L_K, and equation 3 is the partial derivative of the Lagrange multiplier with respect to lambda, L_λ:

$$\underline{\text{Equation 1}}: L_L = 0.2L^{-0.8}K^{0.8} - 9\lambda = 0$$
$$\underline{\text{Equation 2}}: L_K = L^{0.2}0.8K^{-0.2} - 40\lambda = 0$$
$$\underline{\text{Equation 3}}: L_\lambda = 500 - 9L - 40K = 0$$

Now a relationship between L and K is required, and the λ must be removed. First, equation 1 can be multiplied by 40 and equation 2 by 9. This is permissible as it won't affect the relationship between factors in an equation.

$$\underline{\text{Equation 1 (x40)}}: 8L^{-0.8}K^{0.8} - 360\lambda = 0$$
$$\underline{\text{Equation 2 (x9)}}: L^{0.2}7.2K^{-0.2} - 360\lambda = 0$$

Next, new equation 2 can be subtracted from the new equation 1 to remove the λ term, and then the equation can be simplified. Bearing in mind the mathematical rules that a variable can move from one side of a fraction to another by changing the sign of the power, and that multiplying two of the same factors together results in their powers being added together, the result is the relationship between labour, L, and capital, K, to be denoted as equation 4:

$$(8L^{-0.8}K^{0.8} - 360\lambda) - (L^{0.2}7.2K^{-0.2} - 360\lambda) = 0$$
$$8L^{-0.8}K^{0.8} - L^{0.2}7.2K^{-0.2} = 0$$
$$8L^{-0.8}K^{0.8} = L^{0.2}7.2K^{-0.2}$$
$$8L^{-0.8}K^{0.8} / K^{-0.2} = L^{0.2} (7.2)$$
$$8L^{-0.8}K^{0.8+0.2} = 7.2L^{0.2}$$
$$(8)K = 7.2L^{0.2} / L^{-0.8}$$
$$8K = 7.2L^{0.2+0.8}$$
$$8K = 7.2L$$
$$\underline{\text{Equation 4}}: K = 0.9L$$

Equation 4 can then be substituted into equation 3, to give the value of L which will be known as equation 5:

$$\underline{\text{Equation 3}}: 500 - 9L - 40K = 0$$

$$500 - 9L - 40(0.9L) = 0$$
$$500 - 9L - 36L = 0$$
$$500 - 45L = 0$$
$$500 = 45L$$
$$\underline{\text{Equation 5}}: L = 11.111$$

Equation 5 is then substituted into equation 3 to allow the value of K to be calculated, which is equation 6:

$$500 - 9(11.111) - 40K = 0$$
$$400 = 40K$$
$$\text{Equation 6: } K = 10$$

Equation 6 reveals the levels of labour (L) and capital (K) which maximize production to be L = 11.111 units, and K = 10 units. Putting these values into the cost constraint (equation 3) confirms this result. To find the maximum possible output these values can be inserted into the production function for the producer here, $L^{0.2}K^{0.8}$:

$$\text{Maximum output} = (11.111)^{0.2}(10)^{0.8}$$
$$\text{Maximum output} = 10.213 \text{ units}$$

Maximum possible production output for the producer here is 10.213 units.

EXAMPLE 4.2

A producer has the production function $Q = L^{0.5}K^{0.5}$. The producer seeks to minimize costs when the wage rate (w) for labour (L) is £20 per unit, the rental rate (r) for capital (K) is £65 per unit, and the production constraint is 250 units of output (i.e. this number of units is the maximum output the producer expects to be able to sell to consumers, and therefore the maximum they want to produce). Find the levels of labour and capital which minimize costs, and calculate the lowest possible costs.

Answer 4.2

The process for cost minimization is similar to the process just explained for production maximization, in that cost minimization also uses a Lagrange multiplier and is based on constrained optimization. However, with cost minimization the production function becomes part of the constraint instead of being the target of optimization, while the costs of labour at its wage rate (wL) and capital at its rental rate (rK) are optimized instead of being part of the constraint as they were with production maximization.

The optimization function here is costs, C = wL + rK, and is 20L + 65K. The constraint is production function Q = $L^{0.5}K^{0.5}$ where Q is 250, and this is rearranged to remove the equals sign and create a single term: $250 - L^{0.5}K^{0.5}$. Together this gives the following Lagrange multiplier:

$$L = 20L + 65K + \lambda[250 - L^{0.5}K^{0.5}]$$

Cost minimization is like production maximization, as the Lagrange multiplier is partially differentiated with respect to L (L_L), K (L_K), and λ (L_λ), then the results are put equal to zero to optimize them. But the Lagrange multiplier that maximized in the last example can do the opposite and minimize here, as it has production as a constraint and is set up to optimize the levels of labour and capital given their costs (waged labour and rented capital). The three partially differentiated equations that result are:

$$\text{Equation 1: } L_L = 20 - \lambda 0.5 L^{-0.5} K^{0.5} = 0$$
$$\text{Equation 2: } L_K = 65 - \lambda L^{0.5} 0.5 K^{-0.5} = 0$$
$$\text{Equation 3: } L_\lambda = 250 - L^{0.5} K^{0.5} = 0$$

Next, equations 1 and 2 can be used to find the relationship between labour (L) and capital (K). First they can be rearranged to remove the negative sign in each:

$$\text{Equation 1: } \lambda 0.5 L^{-0.5} K^{0.5} = 20$$
$$\text{Equation 2: } \lambda L^{0.5} 0.5 K^{-0.5} = 65$$

Then equation 2 is divided by equation 1 to remove the λ term, before the results are simplified to give the relationship between L and K, denoted as equation 4:

$$(\lambda L^{0.5} 0.5 K^{-0.5} = 65) / (\lambda 0.5 L^{-0.5} K^{0.5} = 20)$$
$$L^{0.5+0.5} K^{-0.5-0.5} = 3.25$$
$$L / K = 3.25$$
$$L = 3.25 K$$
$$\text{Equation 4: } K = L / 3.25$$

Equation 4 can then be substituted into equation 3 (the constraint) which is only made up of L, K and numbers, and the substitution will therefore reveal the numerical value of labour (L) units which minimize costs. This value of L will be known as equation 5:

$$\text{Equation 3: } 250 - L^{0.5}K^{0.5} = 0$$

$$250 - L^{0.5}(L/3.25)^{0.5} = 0$$
$$L^{0.5}L^{0.5} / 3.25^{0.5} = 250$$
$$L / 1.80277 = 250$$
$$\text{Equation 5: } L = 450.69$$

And equation 5 with the value labour, L = 450.69 can be substituted into equation 3 to reveal the value of capital, K, which will be known as equation 6:

$$250 - (450.69)^{0.5}K^{0.5} = 0$$
$$21.229 K^{0.5} = 250$$
$$K^{0.5} = 11.776$$
$$K = 11.776^2$$
$$\text{Equation 6: } K = 138.674$$

Equation 6 reveals the values of labour (L) and capital (K) which minimize the producer's costs to be L = 450.69 units and K = 138.674 units. Putting these values into the production constraint confirms the result. And minimum costs can be calculated by simply putting these L and K values into the cost function, $C = 20L + 65K$:

$$\text{Minimum costs} = 20(450.69) + 65(138.674)$$
$$\text{Minimum costs} = 9{,}013.8 + 9{,}013.81$$
$$\text{Minimum costs} = £18{,}027.61$$

This reveals that the lowest possible costs for the producer here are £18,027.61.

EXERCISES 4

To test understanding of production maximization and cost minimization readers can attempt to answer the following exercise questions, and the methods and solutions to the exercises are presented afterwards:

1. Maximize the production function $Q = L^{1.5}K^2$, when there is a £420 cost constraint, and where the wage rate of labour is £4 per unit, and the rental rate of capital is £8 per unit. Calculate and interpret the maximum output.

2. Minimize costs when there is an £11 wage rate of labour, a £25 rental rate of capital, $Q = 3L^{0.25}K^{0.25}$ is the production function, and there is a production constraint of 200 units of output. Calculate the minimum costs and interpret the results.

SOLUTIONS 4

1. Maximize $Q = L^{1.5}K^2$, subject to $4L + 8K = 420$.

Exercise 1 can be summarized with the above line. The first step is to set up the Lagrange multiplier (L):

$$L = L^{1.5}K^2 + \lambda[420 - 4L - 8K]$$

Next, the Lagrange multiplier is partially differentiated with respect to its three unknown factors; labour with equation 1 L_L, capital with equation 2 L_K, and lambda with equation 3 L_λ. Then each of the 3 equations representing marginal values are put equal to zero to optimize them:

<u>Equation 1</u>: $L_L = 1.5L^{0.5}K^2 - 4\lambda = 0$
<u>Equation 2</u>: $L_K = L^{1.5}2K - 8\lambda = 0$
<u>Equation 3</u>: $L_\lambda = 420 - 4L - 8K = 0$

Now a relationship between L and K must be found by simplifying these equations. One strategy is to multiply equation 1 by 2 so it has the same λ number as equation 2:

<u>Equation 1 (x2)</u>: $3L^{0.5}K^2 - 8\lambda = 0$

And equation 2 can be subtracted from this new equation 1, and then the result can be simplified to reveal the relationship between labour, L, and capital, K. This relationship is denoted below as equation 4:

$$(3L^{0.5}K^2 - 8\lambda) - (L^{1.5}2K - 8\lambda) = 0$$
$$3L^{0.5}K^2 - L^{1.5}2K = 0$$
$$3L^{0.5}K^2 = L^{1.5}2K$$
$$1.5K^{2-1} = L^{1.5-0.5}$$
$$1.5K = L$$
<u>Equation 4</u>: $K = 0.6667L$

Equation 4 is then substituted into equation 3, the constraint, to reveal the value of L which maximizes production. This value is denoted as equation 5:

<u>Equation 3</u>: $420 - 4L - 8K = 0$

$$420 - 4L - 8(0.6667L) = 0$$
$$420 - 4L - 5.333L = 0$$
$$420 - 9.333L = 0$$
$$9.333L = 420$$
<u>Equation 5</u>: $L = 45$

And equation 5 can then be substituted into equation 3 to give the value of capital, K, which maximizes production. This is denoted as equation 6:

$$420 - 4(45) - 8K = 0$$

$$420 - 180 = 8K$$
$$8K = 240$$
<u>Equation 6</u>: $K = 30$

The values of labour, L, and capital, K, which maximize production and output are therefore $L = 45$ units and $K = 30$ units. And the maximum output is calculated by putting the values into the production function, $L^{1.5}K^2$:

Maximum output: $(45)^{1.5}(30)^2$
Maximum output: 271,682.26 units

The maximum possible output here is a huge number, at 271,682.26 units. This is not a mistake, and the value here is far larger than that in example 4.1 for good reason. The production function here exhibits increasing returns to scale (i.e. powers of labour and capital in the production function sum to more than one), and in example 4.1 it only exhibited constant returns to scale (i.e. powers of labour and capital in the production function sum to exactly 1).

2. Minimize costs of $C = 11L + 25K$, subject to the production constraint $Q = 3L^{0.25}K^{0.25} = 200$.

Exercise 2 can be summarized with the previous line. The first step to solve this problem is to set up the Lagrange multiplier (L):

$$L = 11L + 25K + \lambda[200 - 3L^{0.25}K^{0.25}]$$

Then this is partially differentiated with respect to L, K, and λ, and results put equal to zero to optimize them:

Equation 1: $L_L = 11 - \lambda 0.75 L^{-0.75} K^{0.25} = 0$
Equation 2: $L_K = 25 - \lambda 0.75 L^{0.25} K^{-0.75} = 0$
Equation 3: $L_\lambda = 200 - 3L^{0.25} K^{0.25} = 0$

Next, equations 1 and 2 can be rearranged to remove the negative sign in each:

Equation 1: $\lambda 0.75 L^{-0.75} K^{0.25} = 11$
Equation 2: $\lambda 0.75 L^{0.25} K^{-0.75} = 25$

Then equation 2 can be divided by equation 1, and the result can be simplified down to reveal the relationship between L and K, which can be denoted as equation 4:

$$(\lambda 0.75 L^{0.25} K^{-0.75} = 25) / (\lambda 0.75 L^{-0.75} K^{0.25} = 11)$$
$$L^{0.25+0.75} K^{-0.75-0.25} = 2.2727$$
$$L / K = 2.2727$$
$$L = 2.2727K$$
Equation 4: $K = L / 2.2727$

And equation 4 can be substituted into equation 3, the constraint, to give the value of labour, L, which minimizes the producer's costs. This value of L is denoted as equation 5 below:

Equation 3: $200 - 3L^{0.25}K^{0.25} = 0$

$$200 - 3L^{0.25}(L / 2.2727)^{0.25} = 0$$
$$3L^{0.25+0.25} / 2.2727^{0.25} = 200$$
$$3L^{0.5} / 1.2278 = 200$$
$$3L^{0.5} = 245.565$$
$$L^{0.5} = 81.855$$
$$\sqrt{L} = 81.855$$
$$L = 81.855^2$$
Equation 5: $L = 6,700.25$

Equation 5 can then be substituted into equation 3 to give the value of capital, K, which minimizes costs. This value of K is denoted as equation 6:

$$200 - 3(6,700.25)^{0.25}K^{0.25} = 0$$
$$27.142 K^{0.25} = 200$$
$$K^{0.25} = 7.3686$$
$$K = 7.3686^4$$
Equation 6: $K = 2,948.11$

The values of labour, L, and capital, K, which minimize costs for the producer are therefore L = 6,700.25 units, and K = 2,948.11 units. And the minimum possible level of costs can be calculated by putting these values into the cost function, $11L + 25K$:

$$\text{Minimum costs: } 11(6{,}700.25) + 25(2{,}948.11)$$
$$\text{Minimum costs: £}147{,}405.50$$

The minimum possible costs here are £147,405.50, a huge number. This result is basically saying that even the lowest costs for this producer are very high, and as this lowest cost will require thousands of units of labour and capital it's therefore likely that the costs the producer faces will be higher than this value. The cause of these very high costs is the decreasing returns to the production function, where powers sum to less than one (here labour's power is 0.25 and capital's power is also 0.25, summing to 0.5). The message to take from this is that the producer probably shouldn't proceed with the production opportunity here, and when decreasing returns are involved it's often a better idea to search for alternative opportunities.

5 Profit Maximization with Quadratic Equations

If a function takes the form of a quadratic equation, $ax^2 + bx + c = 0$, then a quadratic formula may be needed to optimize it. This section examines such scenarios for the profit functions of perfectly competitive and monopoly firms, and calculates the output level which maximizes firm profits using a quadratic formula, price function, cost function and differentiation.

EXAMPLE 5.1

A perfectly competitive firm faces prices of P = £120. Its total variable costs = $0.5Q^3 - 15Q^2 + 174Q$, total fixed costs = £400. Write equations for the firm's total revenue, total costs, and profit. Calculate maximum and minimum profit and associated output levels. Show that profit is maximized where marginal revenue equals marginal cost.

Answer 5.1

A perfectly competitive firm is a price taker, where its lack of market power prevents it from having any influence over the prices it faces. Instead of price changing with output quantities as in other market structures, the price a perfectly competitive firm faces will be fixed. In this example the price is fixed at P = £120. The price of a product also represents the average revenue (AR) the firm receives, and therefore AR = £120 here. Total revenue (TR) equals average revenue (AR) multiplied by output quantity (Q), TR = AR*Q. Total revenue here equals:

$$\text{Total revenue, TR} = 120Q$$

Total costs (TC) equals the sum of total variable costs (TVC) and total fixed costs (TFC), TC = TVC + TFC. Here total costs therefore equal:

$$\text{Total costs, TC} = \text{TVC} + \text{TFC}$$
$$TC = 0.5Q^3 - 15Q^2 + 174Q + 400$$

Profit (π) is total revenue (TR) minus total costs (TC):

$$\pi = TR - TC$$
$$\pi = 120Q - 0.5Q^3 + 15Q^2 - 174Q - 400$$
$$\pi = -0.5Q^3 + 15Q^2 - 54Q - 400$$

Note that the signs in the total cost function will need to be changed (from − to +, or + to −) to account for the fact that total costs are subtracted in the profit function.

As noted earlier a variable is optimized when its marginal value (its derivative, the change in the variable) equals zero. Therefore the profit function needs to be differentiated and put equal to zero to optimize it and find the output level linked with maximum profits. With only one variable here, Q, there is no need for partial differentiation using several variables and there will only be one way to find the marginal profit, denoted π':

$$\pi = -0.5Q^3 + 15Q^2 - 54Q - 400$$
$$\pi' = -1.5Q^2 + 30Q - 54$$

The quadratic form here means it can't be optimized in the usual way, and the function needs to be resolved with a special quadratic formula. However, because the function is a quadratic a curve of its value would curve one way and then back on itself to create two optimization points: one level of output which gives maximum marginal profit and another which gives minimum marginal profit. The quadratic formula will find both of them, and then it will have to be determined which the (desired) maximum point is and which is the (unwanted) minimum point.

The formula to find maximum and minimum values in a quadratic equation, with form $aQ^2 + bQ + c$, is:

$$Q = [-(b) \pm \sqrt{(b^2 - 4ac)}] / 2a$$

In this example the marginal profit function, $\pi' = -1.5Q^2 + 30Q - 54$, reveals that here 'a' = -1.5, 'b' = 30, and 'c' = -54. Using these values in the formula gives the following results:

$$Q = [-(30) \pm \sqrt{(30^2 - 4(-1.5)(-54))}] / 2(-1.5)$$
$$Q = [-(30) \pm \sqrt{(900 - 324)}] / -3$$
$$Q = [-(30) \pm 24] / -3$$
Either $Q = 2$ with $Q = (-30+24) / -3$
Or $Q = 18$ with $Q = (-30-24) / -3$

The optimizing values of Q are therefore $Q = 2$, and $Q = 18$. It's worth noting that these values could have been found without the quadratic formula, by factorizing the marginal profit equation, $-1.5Q^2 + 30Q - 54$. A little thought reveals the factorization to be $(3-1.5Q)(Q-18)$, and putting each bracket equal to zero individually gives the two optimizing values of Q: $(3-1.5Q) = 0$ gives $1.5Q = 3$ for $Q = 2$, while $(Q-18) = 0$ gives $Q = 18$. However, while this method may be quicker for some, the quadratic formula removes the need to figure out how to factorize what may be a complicated quadratic equation.

The two optimizing values, $Q = 2$ and $Q = 18$, can be separated into a maximum and minimum by examining the second derivative of the profit function, the change of the marginal profit, π''. If the second derivative is positive when one of the Q values is entered into it then the profit is increasing, and as it couldn't increase if at its maximum the point must be a minimum. And if the second derivative is negative then profit is decreasing, and as it couldn't decrease if at its minimum the point must be a maximum.

Marginal profit, π', is the first derivative of profit:

$$\pi' = -1.5Q^2 + 30Q - 54$$

And the derivative of this is the second derivative, π'':

$$\pi'' = -3Q + 30$$

Next, the two optimized values for Q, Q = 2 and Q = 18, are put into this function:

$$\pi'' = -3(2) + 30 = 24$$
$$\pi'' = -3(18) + 30 = -24$$

When output is Q = 2 the $\pi'' = 24$, which is positive to signal profit minimizing. And when output Q = 18 the $\pi'' = -24$, which is negative to signal profit maximizing.

The value of maximum profit can be calculated by putting the value Q = 18 into the profit function:

$$\pi = -0.5Q^3 + 15Q^2 - 54Q - 400$$
$$\pi = -0.5(18)^3 + 15(18)^2 - 54(18) - 400$$
$$\pi = £572$$

Minimum profit is found with Q = 2 in the equation:

$$\pi = -0.5(2)^3 + 15(2)^2 - 54(2) - 400$$
$$\pi = -£452$$

Maximum profit is £572, minimum profit is − £452. The only remaining task is to prove that profit is maximized where marginal revenue (MR) equals marginal costs (MC). MR is the derivative of total revenue, TR = 120Q, and therefore MR = £120. Marginal costs is the derivative of total costs, TC = $0.5Q^3 - 15Q^2 + 174Q + 400$, and therefore MC = $1.5Q^2 - 30Q + 174$. MR will remain the same no matter what the value of Q for a perfectly competitive firm, at £120. With Q = 2 the value of MC = $1.5(2)^2 - 30(2) + 174 = £120$, and with Q = 18 the value of MC = $1.5(18)^2 - 30(18) + 174 = £120$. Therefore profit is maximized where MR = MC, but this condition alone is not enough as it is also minimized where MR = MC. Second derivatives are therefore required to determine the level of Q which is associated with the maximum and not the minimum profit.

EXAMPLE 5.2

A monopolist faces demand of P = 142 − 2Q (i.e. Q = 71 − 0.5P). Total variable costs = $0.5Q^3 - 15Q^2 + 174Q$, and total fixed costs = £250. Write equations for firm total revenue, total costs, and profit. Calculate maximum and minimum profit and the associated output. Show profit is maximized when marginal revenue equals marginal costs.

Answer 5.2

Unlike a perfectly competitive firm a monopolist lacks competition and has market power, and it is a price maker which can influence the prices of its products by changing output (Q) levels. Here price $P = 142 - 2Q$. Price is also average revenue, and $AR = 142 - 2Q$. Total revenue (TR) equals average revenue (AR) multiplied by output quantity (Q), $TR = AR*Q$. Here total revenue equals:

$$\text{Total revenue, } TR = 142Q - 2Q^2$$

Total costs (TC) equals the sum of total variable costs (TVC) and total fixed costs (TFC), $TC = TVC + TFC$:

$$\text{Total costs, } TC = TVC + TFC$$
$$TC = 0.5Q^3 - 15Q^2 + 174Q + 250$$

Profit (π) is total revenue (TR) minus total costs (TC):

$$\pi = TR - TC$$
$$\pi = 142Q - 2Q^2 - 0.5Q^3 + 15Q^2 - 174Q - 250$$
$$\pi = -0.5Q^3 + 13Q^2 - 32Q - 250$$

The derivative of profit, marginal profit π' equals:

$$\pi' = -1.5Q^2 + 26Q - 32$$

Next, the quadratic formula is used, $Q = [-(b) \pm \sqrt{(b^2 - 4ac)}] / 2a$, where a, b, and c are determined by the values of $aQ^2 + bQ + c$ in the marginal profit function. In this example 'a' = – 1.5, 'b' = 26, 'c' = – 32:

$$Q = [-(26) \pm \sqrt{(26^2 - 4(-1.5)(-32))}] / 2(-1.5)$$
$$Q = [-(26) \pm \sqrt{(676 - 192)}] / -3$$
$$Q = [-(26) \pm 22] / -3$$
Either Q = 1.333 with Q = (–26+22) / –3
Or Q = 16 with Q = (–26–22) / –3

The optimizing values of Q are therefore Q = 1.333, and Q = 16. They could have also been found by figuring out how to factorize the marginal profit equation into brackets, (2–1.5Q)(Q–16), and then putting each bracket equal to zero and solving. Using each of the two optimizing values in the second derivative of the profit function will reveal which is a minimum and which is a maximum, and the second derivative of the profit function, π'', is the derivative of marginal profit, π':

$$\pi' = -1.5Q^2 + 26Q - 32$$
$$\pi'' = -3Q + 26$$

Next, the two optimized values for Q, Q = 1.333 and Q = 16, are put into this function:

$$\pi'' = -3(1.333) + 26 = 22$$
$$\pi'' = -3(16) + 26 = -22$$

When output Q = 1.333 the $\pi'' = 22$, which is positive to signal profit minimizing. And when output Q = 16 the value of $\pi'' = -22$, which is negative to signal profit maximizing. Maximum profit can be calculated by putting the value Q = 16 into the profit function, while minimum profit can be calculated with the value Q = 1.333:

$$\pi = -0.5Q^3 + 13Q^2 - 32Q - 250$$
$$\pi = -0.5(16)^3 + 13(16)^2 - 32(16) - 250$$
$$\pi = £518$$

$$\pi = -0.5(1.333)^3 + 13(1.333)^2 - 32(1.333) - 250$$
$$\pi = -£270.74$$

Maximum profit is £518, while minimum profit is – £270.74. It may seem strange that maximum profit for a monopolist is less than that for the perfectly competitive (PC) firm (£572) in the last example. But the monopolist can earn the profit consistently over the long-run, while the PC firm will see new firms enter its industry to eat away the £572 profits until they equal zero in the long-run.

Marginal revenue (MR) is the derivative of total revenue, $TR = 142Q - 2Q^2$, $MR = 142 - 4Q$, while marginal costs are the derivative of total costs, $TC = 0.5Q^3 - 15Q^2 + 174Q + 250$, $MC = 1.5Q^2 - 30Q + 174$. When $Q = 16$ the $MR = MC = £78$, and therefore maximum profit occurs where $MR = MC$. However this condition alone is not enough as minimum profit also occurs where $MR = MC$, and with $Q = 1.333$ the $MR = MC = £136.67$. A negative second derivative of the profit function must be combined with $MR = MC$ to find the profit maximizing Q.

EXERCISES 5

To test understanding of profit maximization for quadratic functions readers can answer the following exercise questions, and the solutions are presented afterwards:

1. A perfectly competitive faces prices of $P = 100$. $TVC = Q^3 - 11Q^2 + 107Q$, and $TFC = 130$. Write equations for TR, TC, and π, and calculate maximum and minimum profit and the associated output.

2. A monopolist faces demand function $P = 167 - Q$ (i.e. $Q = 167 - P$). $TVC = Q^3 - 19Q^2 + 200Q$, and $TFC = 50$. Write equations for TR, TC, and π, and calculate maximum and minimum profit and the associated output.

SOLUTIONS 5

1. P = 100. TVC = $Q^3 - 11Q^2 + 107Q$. TFC = 130

TR = 100Q. TC = $Q^3 - 11Q^2 + 107Q + 130$
$\pi = -Q^3 + 11Q^2 - 7Q - 130$. $\pi' = -3Q^2 + 22Q - 7$
Q = $[-(22) \pm \sqrt{(22^2 - 4(-3)(-7))}] / 2(-3)$
Q = $[-(22) \pm 20] / -6$
Q = 0.333 or 7 to optimize; $(1 - 3Q)(Q - 7)$ factorized
$\pi'' = -6Q + 22$
When Q = 0.333 $\pi'' = 20$, positive for minimum profit
When Q = 7 $\pi'' = -20$, negative for maximum profit
Max profit = £17; Min profit = – £131.15
At max and min profit MR = MC = £100

2. P = 167 – Q. TVC = $Q^3 - 19Q^2 + 200Q$. TFC = 50

TR = $167Q - Q^2$. TC = $Q^3 - 19Q^2 + 200Q + 50$
$\pi = -Q^3 + 18Q^2 - 33Q - 50$; $\pi' = -3Q^2 + 36Q - 33$
Q = $[-(36) \pm \sqrt{(36^2 - 4(-3)(-33))}] / 2(-3)$
Q = $[-(36) \pm 30] / -6$
Q = 1 or 11 to optimize; $(3 - 3Q)(Q - 11)$ factorized
$\pi'' = -6Q + 36$
When Q = 1 $\pi'' = 30$, positive for minimum profit
When Q = 11 $\pi'' = -30$, negative for maximum profit
Max profit = £434; Min profit = – £66
At max, min MR = MC = £165 (Q=1), or £145 (Q=11)

6 Monopoly, Monopolistic Competition, Oligopoly

The equilibrium quantity of output, price, and firm profits can be calculated for firms in different market structures using differentiation and optimization. This section calculates equilibrium and profit maximizing values for monopoly, monopolistically competitive and Cournot oligopoly firms.

EXAMPLE 6.1

A monopolist faces demand function $Q = 170 - P$. The firm's total variable costs $= 10Q$, and total fixed costs $=$ £400. Find the profit maximizing output price and quantity, and the firm's profit.

Answer 6.1

First, the demand function written above in terms of Q must be rearranged into an 'inverse demand function' in terms of P, as a value for P will be needed to find the total revenue, which is part of the profit function. The inverse demand function written in terms of P was given in earlier examples, but it will need to be calculated here, and Q = 170 − P becomes P = 170 − Q.

Next, total revenue (TR) and total costs (TC) are required. TR = AR*Q, where AR is average revenue, and as the price gives average revenue for a firm, AR = P = 170 − Q. This gives total revenue of TR = AR*Q = 170Q − Q^2. Total costs sum total variable costs (TVC) and total fixed costs (TFC), and TVC = 10Q, TFC = 400, gives total costs of TC = 10Q + 400.

Profit (π) = TR − TC = 170Q − Q^2 − 10Q − 400. This simplifies to profit, π = − Q^2 + 160Q − 400. To maximize profit the profit function, π = TR − TC, is differentiated to create marginal profit and then put equal to zero. Differentiating it turns total revenue (TR) and total costs (TC) into marginal revenue (MR) and marginal costs (MC), which turns the TR − TC function into an MR − MC function. When the function is put equal to zero this ensures MR = MC, one of the conditions required for profit maximization. However, as explained in the last section this condition is not enough, as MR = MC also holds when profits are at their minimum. To ensure maximization and not minimization of profits the second derivative of the profit function must also be negative. The first derivative of profit, marginal profit π', and the second derivative of profit, π'', are given below:

$$\pi = -Q^2 + 160Q - 400$$

$$\pi' = -2Q + 160$$
$$\pi'' = -2$$

The second derivative, $\pi'' = -2$, is negative to signal declining profit. This is impossible at a minimum point and must represent profit maximization. Putting marginal profit, π', equal to zero reveals the maximizing quantity:

$$\pi' = -2Q + 160 = 0$$
$$2Q = 160$$
$$Q = 80 \text{ units}$$

And this Q value can be used to find a value for price by entering it into the inverse demand function:

$$P = 170 - (80)$$
$$P = £90$$

And profits are calculated by putting the Q = 80 value into the profit function, $\pi = -Q^2 + 160Q - 400$:

$$\pi = -Q^2 + 160Q - 400$$
$$\pi = -(80)^2 + 160(80) - 400$$
$$\pi = £6,000$$

The monopoly firm here can make a maximum profit of £6,000 by selling 80 units at a price of £90 per unit.

EXAMPLE 6.2

Firms in a monopolistically competitive industry face the inverse demand function $P_i = (15 - Q_i)/N$, where P_i is the price for an individual firm, Q_i is the quantity of units supplied by an individual firm, and N is the number of individual firms in the industry. The cost function for an individual firm in the industry is $C_i = 5 + Q_i$.

Calculate the profit maximizing price, quantity and profit for an individual firm. What is the maximum possible value of N before the profit maximization model breaks down with negative prices or quantities? If profits are driven to zero with free entry of firms into the industry what is the equilibrium number of industry firms?

Answer 6.2

A monopolistically competitive industry is one where firms have the potential to earn monopoly level profits, but where new firms can enter the industry to drive down profits for all as they are divided among more firms. The process to maximize profit is similar to that with monopoly, and first total revenue (TR_i) and total costs (TC_i) for a representative individual firm must be calculated, before the latter is subtracted from the former for individual firm profit, π_i:

$$TR_i = P_i * Q_i = [(15 - Q_i)/N] * Q_i$$
$$TR_i = N^{-1}(15 - Q_i)Q_i$$
$$TR_i = N^{-1}(15Q_i - Q_i^2)$$

$$TC_i = 5 + Q_i$$

$$\pi_i = TR_i - TC_i$$
$$\pi_i = N^{-1}(15Q_i - Q_i^2) - 5 - Q_i$$

Next, the profit function is differentiated (with respect to Q_i) to find marginal profit, π_i', which is then put equal to zero to optimize it. This reveals the profit maximizing value of output, Q_i, for an individual firm given the number of firms (N) in the industry:

$$\pi_i = N^{-1}(15Q_i - Q_i^2) - 5 - Q_i$$
$$\pi_i' = N^{-1}(15 - 2Q_i) - 1 = 0$$
$$(15 - 2Q_i) / N = 1$$
$$15 - 2Q_i = N$$
$$15 = N + 2Q_i$$
$$15 - N = 2Q_i$$
$$Q_i = (15 - N) / 2$$

Note that the derivative of Q_i is 1, as Q_i is really $1Q_i$ and the differentiation removes the Q_i and leaves the 1.

The formula for Q_i is entered into the inverse demand function, P, to reveal a firm's profit maximizing price:

$$P_i = (15 - Q_i)/N$$
$$P_i = (15 - [(15 - N) / 2])/N$$
$$P_iN = 15 - [(15 - N) / 2]$$
$$2P_iN = 30 - (15 - N)$$
$$2P_iN = 15 + N$$
$$P_i = (15 + N) / 2N$$
$$P_i = N^{-1}(15 + N) / 2$$

To find an individual firm's profits, π_i, the formula for Q_i just found could be entered into the profit function which has already been calculated, as per the usual procedure to maximize profit. But given the amount of terms this will create an easier way to find maximum profit is to use the quantity Q_i and price P_i values just found to calculate total revenue and total costs again, and then subtract the latter from the former to find a firm's profit given the level of N:

$$TR_i = P_i * Q_i$$
$$TR_i = [N^{-1}(15 + N) / 2] * [(15 - N) / 2]$$
$$TR_i = [(15 + N) / 2N] * [(15 - N) / 2]$$
$$TR_i = [(15 + N)(15 - N)] / 4N$$

$$TC_i = 5 + Q_i$$
$$TC_i = 5 + [(15 - N) / 2]$$

$$\pi_i = TR_i - TC_i$$

$$\pi_i = [(15 + N)(15 - N)] / 4N - 5 - [(15 - N) / 2]$$
$$\pi_i = (225 - N^2) / 4N - 5 - [(15 - N) / 2]$$
$$\pi_i = [(225 - N^2) - 20N - (30N - 2N^2)] / 4N$$
$$\pi_i = (225 - N^2 - 50N + 2N^2) / 4N$$
$$\pi_i = (N^2 - 50N + 225) / 4N$$
$$\pi_i = (N - 5)(N - 45) / 4N$$

Note that the third line multiplied variables by 4N/4N.

With a profit maximizing output quantity (Q_i) and price (P_i), and a level of profit (π_i) calculated for a firm, the next step is to determine the limitations of this result. If a certain number (N) of firms in the industry results in a negative profit maximizing price or quantity then the equations found will be worthless, as a firm can't set a negative price or produce a negative amount of output, and therefore the price and quantity equations must be examined more closely.

Looking at the price result, $P_i = N^{-1}(15 + N) / 2$, reveals that the profit maximizing price, P_i, will be positive with any value of N. This is visible because N either divides the other factors (N^{-1}), or adds to them (+ N), both of which will give a positive result. Therefore the price result here will hold no matter the number of firms (N) in the industry.

Looking at the output quantity result, $Q_i = (15 - N) / 2$, reveals that N is subtracted in the equation, and therefore a negative result is possible. If N is between 1 and 14 then output quantity Q_i will be a positive number divided by 2, for a positive level of output which a firm could follow. If N was 15 then Q_i would be $0 / 2 = 0$ units, and as a firm could produce zero units of a product $N = 15$ is also a possible result. However, if $N > 15$ then the output quantity required for profit maximization, Q_i, would be a negative number divided by 2, which would give a negative quantity of output. A firm can't produce a negative level of output and therefore the profit maximizing quantity formula will only hold if the number of firms in the industry is less than or equal to 15, $N \leq 15$.

Assuming that the condition $N \leq 15$ holds the equilibrium number of firms in the industry can be calculated using the profit maximizing profit equation, which was $\pi_i = (N - 5)(N - 45) / 4N$. The equilibrium number of firms will be the number of industry firms which is stable, and this will occur when there are no more industry profits available to motivate the entry of additional new firms into the industry. Therefore the equilibrium value of N will occur when there is zero profit available for an individual firm, $\pi_i = 0$.

The profit equation reveals the equilibrium number of industry firms (N) to be 5. With an N value of 5 the first bracket $(N - 5)$ is zero, and this will be multiplied and then divided by the rest of the equation to make the whole equation and profit function, π_i, zero too.

EXAMPLE 6.3

A Cournot oligopoly sees two firms compete on the amount of output they produce, and output decisions are reactions to their independent expectations of other firms' output levels. Each firm has the demand function $Q = 64 - P$, where Q is the total industry output combining the quantity of output for both firm 1 (q_1) and firm 2 (q_2) in the two firm duopoly, and $Q = q_1 + q_2$. The cost function for each individual firm is $C_i = 12 + 2q_i$, where q_i is q_1 for firm 1 and q_2 for firm 2. Find the reaction functions, price, quantity and profit for each of the Cournot competitors.

Answer 6.3

The first step is to turn the demand function here written in terms of Q into an inverse demand function written in terms of P, as a value for P will be needed to find total revenue, which is part of the profit function. Simple rearranging turns the $Q = 64 - P$ demand function into inverse function $P = 64 - Q$, which is $P = 64 - q_1 - q_2$.

Next, total revenue (TR) and total cost (TC) functions are required for each firm. Firm 1's total revenue equals the price they face, $P = 64 - q_1 - q_2$, multiplied by the quantity they produce, q_1. The result is $TR_1 = (64 - q_1 - q_2)q_1 = 64q_1 - q_1^2 - q_1q_2$. And firm 1's total costs are the cost function, $C_i = 12 + 2q_i$, applied to their own output for

$TC_1 = 12 + 2q_1$. The profit for firm 1, π_1, is firm 1's total revenue minus their total costs:

$$\pi_1 = 64q_1 - q_1^2 - q_1q_2 - 12 - 2q_1$$
$$\pi_1 = 62q_1 - q_1^2 - q_1q_2 - 12$$

And this is differentiated with respect to firm 1's output, q_1, to give firm's 1 marginal profit, π_1', which is put equal to zero to optimize it for firm 1's profit maximization. But the derivative of marginal profit, which is the second derivative of profit with respect to q_1, π_1'', must also be calculated to ensure that the optimization process will find a maximum and not a minimum:

$$\pi_1' = 62 - 2q_1 - q_2 = 0$$
$$62 - q_2 = 2q_1$$
$$q_1 = 31 - 0.5q_2$$

$$\pi_1' = 62 - 2q_1 - q_2 = 0$$
$$\pi_1'' = -2$$

The second derivative of profit, π_1'', is negative and the optimization process will find a point of maximum profit as hoped, and not a point of minimum profit.

The calculated q_1 value, $q_1 = 31 - 0.5q_2$, is known as firm 1's reaction function, and under Cournot competition firm 1 will react to firm 2's output with its own output based on the relationship shown. As firm 1 and firm 2 are in the same position the reaction function for firm 2 will be the same as for firm 1, except that q_1 and q_2 positions will switch around:

$$q_2 = 31 - 0.5q_1$$

With reaction functions for both firm 1 and for firm 2 one can be substituted into the other, to turn q_1 and q_2 from reaction functions into specific values of output quantity. Substituting the q_2 formula into the q_1 formula gives:

$$q_1 = 31 - 0.5(31 - 0.5q_1)$$
$$q_1 = 31 - 15.5 + 0.25q_1$$
$$0.75q_1 = 15.5$$
$$q_1 = 20.667 \text{ units}$$

And this q_1 value is substituted into firm 2's reaction function, $q_2 = 31 - 0.5q_1$, for a q_2 value. The result is the same as for firm 1, as both firms are in the same position:

$$q_2 = 31 - 0.5q_1$$
$$q_2 = 31 - 0.5(20.667)$$
$$q_2 = 20.667 \text{ units}$$

$q_1 = q_2 = 20.667$ units of output is the equilibrium quantity for the two firms in Cournot competition, and this value can be entered into the price (i.e. inverse demand) function to reveal the equilibrium price:

$$P = 64 - q_1 - q_2$$
$$P = 64 - (20.667) - (20.667)$$
$$P = £22.667$$

The equilibrium price for both Cournot competitors is £22.667. And entering the q_1 and q_2 values into firm 1's profit function, π_1, will reveal the Cournot competitor's profit:

$$\pi_1 = 62q_1 - q_1^2 - q_1q_2 - 12$$
$$\pi_1 = 62(20.667) - (20.667)^2 - (20.667)(20.667) - 12$$
$$\pi_1 = £415.11$$

Firm 1's profit, π_1, is £415.11. And as both firms are in the same position firms 2's profit is also £415.11.

EXERCISES 6

To test understanding of profit maximizing and equilibrium solutions for monopoly, monopolistically competitive and Cournot oligopoly market structures readers can answer the following exercise questions, and the solutions to the exercises are presented afterwards:

1. A monopolist has demand function $Q = 600 - 0.667P$. $TVC = 0$, and $TFC = 11,250$. Find the profit maximizing price and quantity for the firm, and calculate the monopolist's profits.

2. Firms in a monopolistically competitive industry each face the demand function $P_i = (120 - 2Q_i)/N$, where P_i and Q_i relate to an individual firm's price and quantity of output supply, and N is the number of firms in the industry. Costs, $C_i = 25 + 2Q_i$ for each firm. Calculate the profit maximizing price and quantity for an individual firm and their profits when $N = 4$, and then repeat the process when $N = 10$.

3. A Cournot oligopoly sees two firms compete on the amount of output they produce, and firms base their output decisions on their independent expectations of other firms' output. Each firm has the consumer demand function $Q = 50 - 2P$, where Q is the total industry output which combines output for both firm 1 (q_1) and firm 2 (q_2) in the two firm duopoly, $Q = q_1 + q_2$. The cost function for each firm is $C_i = 20 + qi$, where qi is $q1$ for firm 1 and $q2$ for firm 2. Find the reaction functions, equilibrium price and quantity, and the profit for each firm.

SOLUTIONS 6

1. $Q = 600 - 0.667P$. $TVC = 0$. $TFC = 11{,}250$

$Q = 600 - 0.667P$ becomes $P = 900 - 1.5Q$
$P = AR = 900 - 1.5Q$. $TR = AR*Q = 900Q - 1.5Q^2$
$TC = TVC + TFC = 0 + 11{,}250 = 11{,}250$
$\pi = TR - TC = 900Q - 1.5Q^2 - 11{,}250$
$\pi' = 900 - 3Q = 0$
$3Q = 900$
Profit maximizing $Q = 300$ units
Check second derivative of profit function for a max:
$\pi'' = -3$, negative for profit maximizing
Put calculated value of Q into price function:
$P = 900 - 1.5Q$
$P = 900 - 1.5(300)$
Profit maximizing price $P = £450$
Put value of Q into profit function:
$\pi = 900Q - 1.5Q^2 - 11{,}250$
$\pi = 900(300) - 1.5(300)^2 - 11{,}250$
Maximum profit $\pi = £123{,}750$

2. $P_i = (120 - 2Q_i)/N$. $C_i = 25 + 2Q_i$. $N = 4$ or $N = 10$.

This question is a little different to the earlier example for monopolistically competitive firms, as that didn't give a specific value for N but this exercise does. First, total revenue is found by multiplying price (P_i) by quantity (Q_i): $TR_i = P_i * Q_i = [(120 - 2Q_i)/N]*Q_i = N^{-1}120Q_i - 2Q_i^2$. The cost function, $C_i = 25 + 2Q_i$, reveals that total costs $TC_i = 25 + 2Q_i$ (i.e. total fixed costs of 25, and total variable costs of $2Q_i$). Profit, π_i, is total revenue minus total costs and here this equals:

$$\pi_i = N^{-1}120Q_i - 2Q_i^2 - 25 - 2Q_i$$

Profit is differentiated to give marginal profit, π_i', and put equal to zero to find the Q_i value which optimizes it:

$$\pi_i' = N^{-1}120 - 4Q_i - 2 = 0$$
$$(120 / N) - 2 = 4Q_i$$
$$Q_i = (30 / N) - 0.5$$
$$\textbf{(If N = 4)}\ Q_i = (30 / 4) - 0.5 = 7$$
$$\textbf{(If N = 10)}\ Q_i = (30 / 10) - 0.5 = 2.5$$

And the negative second derivative of the profit function, π_i'', shows that these optimizing values of Q_i will maximize and not minimize an individual firm's profit:

$$\pi_i'' = -4$$

Using the two Q_i values, 7 when $N = 4$, and 2.5 when $N = 10$, in the price function gives the equilibrium price:

$$P_i = (120 - 2Q_i)/N$$

(If N = 4) $P_i = (120 - 2(7))/4$
$P_i = (106)/4$
$P_i = £26.50$
(If N = 10) $P_i = (120 - 2(2.5))/10$
$P_i = (115)/10$
$P_i = £11.50$

And substituting the two Q_i values, 7 when N = 4, and 2.5 when N = 10, into the profit function will reveal an individual firm's profit, π_i:

$$\pi_i = N^{-1}120Q_i - 2Q_i^2 - 25 - 2Q_i$$

(If N = 4) $\pi_i = [120(7) / 4] - 2(7)^2 - 25 - 2(7)$
$\pi_i = £73$
(If N = 10) $\pi_i = [120(2.5) / 4] - 2(2.5)^2 - 25 - 2(2.5)$
$\pi_i = £32.50$

With 4 firms in the monopolistically competitive industry (N = 4) an individual firm's profit maximizing price is £26.50, output quantity is 7 units, and profits are £73. But 10 firms in the monopolistically competitive industry (N = 10) sees profits shared among more firms and all the values fall, and a firm's profit maximizing price is £11.50, output quantity is 2.5 units, and profit is £32.50.

3. $Q = 50 - 2P$. $C_i = 20 + q_i$

$Q = 50 - 2P$ is rearranged for inverse demand function $P = 25 - 0.5Q$, which gives $P = 25 - 0.5(q_1 + q_2)$, $P = 25 - 0.5q_1 - 0.5q_2$

Firm 1 $TR_1 = P*q_1 = 25q_1 - 0.5q_1^2 - 0.5q_1q_2$
Firm 1 $TC_1 = 20 + q_1$
Firm 1 $\pi_1 = 25q_1 - 0.5q_1^2 - 0.5q_1q_2 - 20 - q_1$
Firm 1 $\pi_1 = 24q_1 - 0.5q_1^2 - 0.5q_1q_2 - 20$
Firm 1 max profit $\pi_1' = 24 - q_1 - 0.5q_2 = 0$
Rearrange π_1' for firm 1 output reaction function, q_1:
$24 - q_1 - 0.5q_2 = 0$
$q_1 = 24 - 0.5q_2$
And firm 2's reaction function is the mirror of this:
$q_2 = 24 - 0.5q_1$

Check second derivative of profit function before searching for optimizing values to ensure they will give a point of maximum and not minimum profit:

$\pi'' = -1$, negative to show a trend of declining profit, and as profit can't decline if at a minimum the point is confirmed as a point of profit maximization

Then combine the two reaction functions, q_1 and q_2 to find a specific value of q_1:
$q_1 = 24 - 0.5(24 - 0.5q_1)$
$q_1 = 24 - 12 + 0.25q_1$
$0.75q_1 = 12$
Equilibrium and profit maximizing $q_1 = 16$ units

And as firm 1 and firm 2 are in the same position, the equilibrium and profit maximizing q_2 = 16 units

The $q_1 = q_2 = 16$ value is put into the price function (inverse demand function) to give the equilibrium price value which will hold for both Cournot competitors:

$P = 25 - 0.5q_1 - 0.5q_2$
$P = 25 - 0.5(16) - 0.5(16)$
$P = £9$

And the $q_1 = 16$ value can be put into firm 1's profit function, π_1, to calculate profit:

$\pi_1 = 24q_1 - 0.5q_1^2 - 0.5q_1q_2 - 20$
$\pi_1 = 384 - 128 - 128 - 20$
Profit for firm 1, $\pi = £108$

And as firm 2 is in exactly the same position firm 2's profit under Cournot competition will also be £108.

7 Asymmetric Information

The negative consequences of asymmetric information on buyer and seller outcomes can be calculated by comparing actual, equilibrium, and efficient results.

EXAMPLE 7.1

There are 101 people selling used phones which all vary in their individual quality. The quality of the used phones is uniformly distributed from 0 up to 100, and one phone has a 0 quality, one phone has a 1 quality, … , and one phone has a 100 quality. Every seller knows the precise value of their phone, and wants to do everything they can to sell it.

Buyers know that overall the phones vary in quality from 0 to 100 units in quality. However, buyers face a problem as they don't know the precise quality of an individual phone until after they've bought it, and every seller will naturally claim that their own phone is of the highest quality in order to sell it, yet this can't be true of every phone. Due to their lack of information on individual phone quality buyers can do no more than estimate it, using the average quality of all the used phones.

Sellers will only be willing to sell their phone if the price they are offered matches or exceeds its quality, and at a price of £P a seller will only sell their phone if its quality is P units or less. Buyers are willing to pay a price which exceeds the quality of a phone, and will pay up to price £P for a phone with quality of P − 10 units. For example, buyers would be willing to pay £10 for a phone with a quality of 0, and £70 for a phone with a 60 quality.

(i) If all 101 used phones are for sale what price would buyers be willing to pay for a phone? At this price how many and which owners would be willing to sell their used phones? Is this an equilibrium?

(ii) If all phones up to quality Q are for sale, with Q between 0 and 100 and normally distributed, then what price will buyers pay for a used phone? Which owners will sell their phones at this price? Find the equilibrium price and quantity. Is this outcome efficient?

Answer 7.1

(i) The example explains that buyers will be willing to pay a price 10 units higher than a phone's quality, as they will pay price P for a phone with quality P − 10. But of course the buyer doesn't know the individual quality of a phone, and they can only estimate it based on the average quality of all phones, which is the only information they possess.

101 used phones for sale means the average phone would be the (101 + 1) / 2 = 51st phone, and a 1 is added to the 101 number before dividing it by 2 as 101 is an odd number. Applying the uniform distribution of phone values, 0 to 100, to the 101 phones means that the 1st phone has a quality of 0, the 2nd phone has a quality of 1, … , and the 101st phone has a quality of 100. Following this principle that the quality of a phone is its number minus 1 means that the 51st and average used phone would have a quality of 50. As buyers will pay a price of P for a phone with quality $P - 10$, and the average phone value of 50 represents quality of '$P - 10$' here, the price P that a buyer will be willing to pay can be found as follows:

$$P - 10 = 50$$
$$P = £60$$

A buyer will be willing to pay £60 for a used phone when they lack information on its individual quality. It was noted in the example that an owner of the used phone would only sell their phone if they received a price which matched or exceeded its true quality. Therefore if a buyer is willing to pay £60 for a used phone then only sellers with a phone quality of 60 or less will make the trade. Returning to the idea that a phone's quality is its number minus 1 here, if only phone sellers with a phone quality of 60 or less will sell their phone then only 61 of the 101 used phone owners will be willing to sell their phone given the price that buyers offer them. This leaves 40 of the 101 used phone sellers, roughly 40% of the total, who end up not selling their phone to phone buyers.

As all 101 used phone owners will sell their phone as long as they get a price which at least meets its quality, and as all buyers are willing to pay a price for a phone which exceeds its quality (by as much as 10), it is possible for all 101 phone sellers to sell their phones to buyers. This would leave 101 sellers and 101 buyers happy and would be an equilibrium outcome. Therefore the situation here where 101 phone sellers intend to sell their phone but only 61 manage to sell their phone is not an equilibrium outcome. 40 phone sellers and 40 phone buyers will be left unsatisfied, and all because of asymmetric information where buyers can't be sure of the true quality and value of an individual phone, while sellers are unable to prove their phone's true quality and value to buyers.

(ii) If all used phones up to quality of level Q are for sale, and if quality is uniformly distributed, then the average quality of a used phone is $Q/2$. It has already been noted that buyers will pay price P for a $P - 10$ quality phone, and to find the price they would pay for an average quality phone, $Q/2$, this value is simply seen as $P - 10$:

$$P - 10 = Q/2$$
$$P = Q/2 + 10$$

Buyers would pay £(Q/2 + 10) for a phone of quality Q/2. At this price only sellers whose phones had quality of Q or less (i.e. they intend to sell their phone), and quality of Q/2 + 10 or less (i.e. their phone's quality is met by the buyer's price) will sell their phone.

At the equilibrium all those selling their phone (sellers with phones up to quality Q) will manage to sell their phone, by getting the price they require. As buyers only offer £(Q/2 + 10) only sellers with phone quality (Q/2 + 10) or less will get the price they require. Therefore at the equilibrium Q (those with phones for sale) = Q/2 + 10 (those who manage to sell). This reveals the value of Q:

$$Q = Q/2 + 10$$
$$Q = 0.5Q + 10$$
$$0.5Q = 10$$
$$Q = 20$$

The equilibrium occurs with a phone quality of 20, and price of £(Q/2 + 10) = £(20/2 + 10) = £20. This is not efficient, and when only the phones up to quality Q are for sale only 1/5 of them sell (21 out of 101, as a value of 20 corresponds to the 21st used phone if a uniform distribution is assumed). With buyers always placing a higher value on used phones than sellers every phone should sell, at a price between the buyer and seller valuation. But asymmetric information and a seller's inability to demonstrate phone quality and a buyer's inability to determine phone quality prevents the efficient outcome, leaving an inefficient one.

EXERCISES 7

To test understanding of asymmetric information readers can answer the following exercise question, and the solution is presented afterwards:

There are 1,501 people selling used cars which all vary in their individual quality. The quality of the used cars is uniformly distributed from 0 up to 1,500, and one car has a 0 quality, one car has a 1 quality, ... , and one car has a 1,500 quality. Every seller knows the precise quality of their used car, and they want to do everything they can to sell it.

Buyers know that overall the used cars vary in quality from 0 to 1,500 units of quality. However, buyers face a problem as they don't know the precise quality of an individual car until after they've bought it, and every seller will naturally claim that their own car is of the highest quality in order to sell it, yet this can't be true of every car. Due to their lack of information on individual used car quality buyers can do no more than estimate it, using the average quality of all the used cars.

Sellers will only be willing to sell their used car if the price they are offered matches or exceeds its quality, and at a price of £P a seller will only sell their car if its quality is P units or less. Buyers are willing to pay a price which exceeds the quality of a car, and will pay up to price £P for a car with quality of P – 500 units. For example, buyers would be willing to pay £500 for a car with a quality of 0 units, and £1,500 for a car with a 1,000 quality.

(i) If all 1,501 used cars are for sale what price would buyers be willing to pay for a car? At this price how many and which owners would be willing to sell their used cars? Is this an equilibrium?

(ii) If all cars up to quality Q are for sale, with Q between 0 and 1,500, then what price will buyers pay for a used car? Which car owners will sell at this price? Find the equilibrium price and quantity and explain if this outcome is efficient or not.

SOLUTIONS 7

1 (i) Buyers only know the average and not individual car quality. With 1,501 used cars, $(1,501 + 1) / 2 = 751^{st}$ car is the average one. A uniform distribution of 0 to 1,500 quality for cars 1 to 1,501 means that the average 751st car has average quality 750. Buyers will pay price P for a P – 500 quality car, and the 750 average quality represents the P – 500, and $750 = P - 500$. Therefore $P = 750 + 500 =$ £1,250, and buyers will pay £1,250 for a used car.

Only car sellers with a car quality of 1,250 or less will sell their car, and only number 1 to 1,251 used car sellers will sell their car. The other 250 (from 1,251 to 1,501) won't sell their car as they don't get a price which matches its quality. With all cars for sale but one sixth (250 out of 1,501) cars not selling the result is not an equilibrium.

(ii) Average quality is Q/2. Buyers will pay £(Q/2 + 500) for a car, and only sellers whose car both has a quality of Q or less (so car is for sale), and whose quality is Q/2 + 500 or less (so would sell), will sell their used car. At equilibrium those whose cars are for sale will sell them, and $Q = Q/2 + 500$, therefore $Q = 0.5Q + 500$, $0.5Q = 500$, $Q = 1,000$. Price, $P = Q/2 + 500 = £1,000$. This price of £1,000 and quality of 1,000 is not an efficient outcome, as only the first 1,001 used car sellers will sell their car, and the rest of the 1,501 car sellers (1/3, or 500 sellers) won't sell it. An efficient outcome would see all cars sell.

www.ingramcontent.com/pod-product-compliance
Lightning Source LLC
Chambersburg PA
CBHW051732170526
45167CB00002B/909